SERIES TEACHING FILM

Teaching
Men and Film

Matthew Hall

Series Editor: Vivienne Clark
Commissioning Editor: Wendy Earle

bfi Education

British Library Cataloguing–in–Publication Data
A catalogue record for this guide is available in the British Library

ISBN 1 84457 082 7

First published in 2005 by the British Film Institute
21 Stephen Street, London W1T 1LN

Design: Amanda Hawkes
Cover photograph: *Fight Club* – courtesy of *bfi* Stills
Printed in Great Britain by: Cromwell Press Ltd

www.bfi.org.uk

The British Film Institute's purpose is to champion moving image culture
in all its richness and diversity across the UK, for the benefit of as wide
an audience as possible, and to create and encourage debate.

Contents

Introduction to the series

Since the introduction of the revised post-16 qualifications (AS and A2 Level) in the UK in September 2000, the number of students taking A Level Film and Media Studies has increased significantly. For example, the latest entry statistics show the following trend:

Subject & Level	June 2001	June 2002	June 2004
A Level Film Studies†	2,017	—	—
AS Level Film Studies	3,852	—	7,996
A2 Level Film Studies	—	2,175	4,161
A Level Media Studies*†	16,293	—	—
AS Level Media Studies*	22,872	—	30,745
A2 Level Media Studies*	—	18,150	22,746

*Three combined awarding bodies' results
† Legacy syllabi – last entry June 2001
(*bfi* Education website – AS/A2 statistics refer to cashed-in entries only)

In September 2006, a new A Level specification (syllabus), Moving Image Arts (offered by the Northern Ireland awarding body, CCEA), will be available throughout the UK and it is likely to attract even more students to this lively and popular subject area. We will be adding reference to it in the Assessment contexts section of the forthcoming titles in the series.

Inevitably this increase in student numbers has led to a pressing demand for more teachers. But, given the comparatively recent appearance of both subjects at degree level (and limited availability of specialist post-graduate teaching courses), both new and experienced teachers from other disciplines are faced with teaching these subjects for the first time, without a degree-level background to help them with subject content and conceptual understanding.

In addition, these specifications saw the arrival of new set topics and areas of study, some of which change frequently, so there is a pressing need for up-to-date resources to help teacher preparation, as well as continuing professional development courses.

I meet a large number of Film and Media Studies teachers every year in the course of my various roles and developed the concept and format of this series with the above factors, and busy and enthusiastic teachers, in mind. Each title provides an accessible reference resource, with essential topic content, as well as clear guidance on good classroom practice to improve the quality of teaching and students' learning. We are confident that, as well as supporting the teacher new to these subjects, the series provides the experienced specialist with new critical perspectives and teaching approaches as well as useful content.

The two sample schemes of work in Section 1 are intended as practical models to help get teachers started. They are not prescriptive, as any effective scheme of work has to be developed with the specific requirements of an assessment context, and ability of the teaching group, in mind. Likewise, the worksheets provided in the online materials offer examples of good practice, which can be adapted to your specific needs and contexts. In some cases, the online resources include additional resources, such as interviews and illustrative material, available as webnotes. See www.bfi.org.uk/tfms.

The series is clear evidence of the range, depth and breadth of teacher expertise and specialist knowledge required at A Level in these subjects. Also, it is an affirmation of why this subject area is such an important, rich and compelling one for increasing numbers of 16- to 19-year-old students. Many of the more theoretical titles in the series include reference to practical exercises involving media production skills. It is important that it is understood here that the current A Levels in Media and Film Studies are not designed as vocational, or pre-vocational, qualifications. In these contexts, the place of practical media production is to offer students active, creative and engaging ways in which to explore theory and reflect on their own practice.

It has been very gratifying to see that the first titles in this series have found an international audience, in the USA, Canada and Australia, among others, and we hope that future titles continue to be of interest in international moving image education.

Every author in the series is an experienced practitioner of Film and/or Media Studies at this level and many have examining/moderating experience. It has been a pleasure to work closely with such a diverse range of committed professionals and I should like to thank them for their individual contributions to this expanding series.

Vivienne Clark
Series Editor
July 2005

● Key features

- Assessment contexts for the major UK post-16 Film and Media Studies specifications
- Suggested schemes of work
- Historical contexts (where appropriate)
- Key facts, statistics and terms
- Detailed reference to the key concepts of Film and Media Studies
- Detailed case studies
- Glossaries
- Bibliographies
- Student worksheets, activities and resources (available online) – ready for you to print and photocopy for the classroom

● Other titles available in the series include:

Teaching Scriptwriting, Screenplays and Storyboards for Film & TV Production – Mark Readman
Teaching TV Sitcom – James Baker
Teaching Digital Video Production – Pete Fraser and Barney Oram
Teaching TV News – Eileen Lewis
Teaching Women and Film – Sarah Gilligan
Teaching World Cinema – Kate Gamm
Teaching TV Soaps – Lou Alexander and Alison Cousens
Teaching Contemporary British Broadcasting – Rachel Viney
Teaching Contemporary British Cinema – Sarah Casey Benyahia
Teaching Music Video – Pete Fraser
Teaching Auteur Study – David Wharton and Jeremy Grant

● Forthcoming titles include:

Teaching Analysis of Film Language; *Teaching Video Games*; *Teaching Film Censorship and Controversy*; *Teaching Stars and Performance*; *Teaching TV Drama*; *Teaching Short Films.*

SERIES EDITOR: Vivienne Clark is a former Head of Film and Media Studies and an Advanced Skills Teacher. She is currently an Associate Tutor of *bfi* Education and Principal Examiner for A Level Media Studies for one of the English awarding bodies. She is a freelance teacher trainer, media consultant and writer/editor, with several published textbooks and resources, including *GCSE Media Studies* (Longman 2002), *Key Concepts & Skills for Media Studies* (Hodder Arnold 2002). She is also a course tutor for the *bfi*/Middlesex University MA Level module, An Introduction to Media Education and a link tutor and visiting lecturer for the Central School of Speech & Drama PGCE (Media with English), London.

AUTHOR: Matthew Hall is Head of Film and Media Studies at Seven Kings High School in Essex, where he delivers GCSE, AS and A2 Level Media Studies. He has an MA in Postmodernism and Contemporary Culture, and has run workshops on Youth Subculture Theory at the *bfi* Media Studies Conference.

1

Introduction

Assessment contexts

Awarding Body & Level	Subject	Unit Code	Module/Topic
✓ AQA AS Level	Media Studies	Med1	Reading the Media
✓ AQA AS Level	Media Studies	Med2	Textual Topics in Contemporary Media
✓ AQA A2 Level	Media Studies	Med4	Texts and Contexts in Media
✓ AQA A2 Level	Media Studies	Med5	Independent Study
✓ AQA A2 Level	Media Studies	Med6	Comparative Critical Analysis
✓ OCR AS Level	Media Studies	2731	Textual Analysis
✓ OCR A2 Level	Media Studies	2735	Media Issues and Debates
✓ OCR A2 Level	Media Studies	2734	Critical Research Study
✓ OCR A2 Level	Media Studies	2733	Advanced Production
✓ WJEC A2 Level	Film Studies	FS4	Making Meaning 2
✓ WJEC A2 Level	Film Studies	FS5	Studies in World Cinema
✓ WJEC A2 Level	Film Studies	FS6	Critical Studies
✓ WJEC A2 Level	Media Studies	MS2	Media Representations and Reception
✓ WJEC A2 Level	Media Studies	MS4	Investigating Media Texts
✓ SQA Higher	Media Studies	D332 13	Media Analysis
✓ SQA Higher	Media Studies	D37A 13	Media Investigation
✓ CCEA AS Level	Moving Image Arts	AS1	Language
✓ CCEA AS Level	Moving Image Arts	AS3	Conceptual Framework: Context

This guide is also relevant to the following specifications, as well as to international and Lifelong Learning courses.

- AQA, Ed-Excel, OCR – GNVQ and AVCE Media and Communication
- BTEC National Diploma

Other guides in this series offer excellent complementary information to this guide:

- *Teaching World Cinema* – Kate Gamm
- *Teaching Women and Film* – Sarah Gilligan
- *Teaching Auteur Studies* – David Wharton and Jeremy Grant
- *Teaching Analysis of Film Language* – David Wharton and Jeremy Grant
- *Teaching Film Censorship and Controversy* – Mark Readman

● AQA A Level Media Studies

Module 1 – Reading the Media
- The use of close textual analysis skills to look at representations of gender in children's adverts.

Module 2 – Textual Topics in Contemporary Media
- Discussion of the representation of gender in films compared with audience reactions. Do men and women view gender representations differently?

Module 4 – Texts and Contexts in Media
- Representations of men and male issues: What are dominant views of masculinity? What are alternative views? Is the gender of a director significant?
- Genre and media audiences: Are there male film genres? If so, what are they? Are male audiences attracted to clearly identified genres?

Module 5 – Independent Study
- Use either focus films or directors to investigate their treatment of masculinity as a theme, and their relationship with audiences. Note: ensure that the principal focus texts meet the criteria of 'contemporary', as defined by AQA.

Module 6 – Comparative Critical Analysis
- Comparing representations of men in the same genre but from different times (eg a Western and *RoboCop*); comparing representations of homosexuality in Todd Haynes' films and romantic comedies; comparing representations of men in mainstream and alternative cinema.

● OCR A Level Media Studies

2731 – Textual Analysis
- Examine gender stereotypes and how they are reinforced or challenged in film as a contrast to TV sitcoms; or consider how representations of men and women are used to target a traditional/modern male audience.

2735 – Media Issues and Debates
- Film censorship – eg Verhoeven's use of explicit sex and violence to explore male desires; *Fight Club* controversy; offensive images of women and men in film.

2734 – Critical Research Study
- Women and Film topic – do female and male audiences differ in their responses to films?
- Children and TV topic – younger male and female audiences; ideas about gender and scopophilia be applied to TV.

2733 – Advanced Production
- Use knowledge of male audiences to create a media product aimed at this market.

● WJEC A Level Film Studies

FS4 – Making Meaning 2
- Auteur research project – Todd Haynes, Paul Verhoeven.

FS5 – Studies in World Cinema
- Todd Haynes and the New Queer cinema.
- Compare representations of masculinity in American, Russian and Mexican films.

FS6 – Critical Studies
- Feminist film theory.
- Link to study of social change in relation to film production and reception.

● WJEC A Level Media Studies

MS2 – Media Representations and Reception
- Representation of men and how different gender audiences react.

MS4 – Investigating Media Texts
- Comparing representations of men from different cultures; comparing gay and heterosexual directors' views of masculinity.

- ## SQA Higher/Advanced Higher Media Studies

D332 13 Media Analysis
- Application of film theory to texts – Mulvey, postmodernism.

D37A 13 Media Investigation
- Audiences and consumption – What attracts male audiences? How do they respond to specific content?
- Representation of gender.

- ## CCEA AS Level Moving Image Arts

AS1 – Language
- How different techniques are used to produce different representations of men and women

AS3 – Conceptual Framework: Context
- How do male and female audiences interpret films differently?
- How are men and women (and associated issues) represented in films?

Rationale – Why study 'Men and Film'?

The changing status of the female in society since the 1960s has been widely documented, but in the wake of feminist thought a clearly identifiable body of popular and academic writing has emerged which offers a masculinist perspective on the roles and functions of men in contemporary society and, indeed, its own ripostes to feminism in its various forms.

The financial independence of women, equal opportunities legislation, the rising divorce rate, the re-positioning of gay culture into the mainstream – these, and many other socio-economic and cultural forces, have made any contemporary consensus on the attributes of a 'real' man, somewhat elusive. As a direct consequence of feminism, in the past 15 years, we can see an increasing interest in definitions of masculinity, as students of contemporary politics and popular culture have turned their attention to deconstructing and reconstructing masculinity for a variety of political, artistic and commercial purposes. A recent book called *The Many Faces of Men* (Stephen Whitehead, 2004) claims to assist women in understanding men by isolating 27 different types, from the 'gadget-man' to the 'emotional backpacker'. John Gray asserts that 'Men are from Mars …', and have not advanced emotionally from their Neolithic caves. However, I would argue that the range of masculine roles presented to us via the mass media, and other cultural forms, is now far more varied than any simplifying (and self-serving) self-help manual can suggest, and, in particular, that these roles have been explored in a number of ways by the cinema of the past 20 years.

Have men changed? Or just the way society sees them? Is there a 'crisis in masculinity', as has been widely claimed? By looking at the media – from advertising Calvin Klein perfume, to the global marketing of a living 'brand', David Beckham – we can see there is no real cohesion to the changes in masculinity. Men, and their own individual ideas of what a man actually is, are so varied in the 21st century that generalisations are impossible to make. Are all men now 'metrosexual': quite comfortable with buying moisturiser, happy to visit a gay nightclub with female friends and able to articulate their complex emotional states? Or is this version of masculinity a construct of consumerism, whereby men have now become a new market for a whole plethora of products? A flick through magazines like *Nuts* – which seems to target the most stereotypical of lads with features about racing cars, binge-drinking and porn stars – reveals adverts for hair-gel, eyedrops and moisturising shaving gel. Even within these critically reviled 'lads' mags' the messages about masculinity are complex and ambiguous.

An alternative view is that the postmodern man isn't 'real', that men have lost touch with their 'core' masculinity. 'Is that what a real man looks like?' smirks Brad Pitt's Tyler Durden in *Fight Club* (David Fincher, USA, 1999) at a beautified male model on a perfume advert. Certainly – and as will be discussed in more detail later – the characters in *Fight Club* feel that the 'real' man has been lost amongst the dazzling images produced by capitalism and the media. Yet, when the layers of 'fake' masculinity have finally been stripped away, what does the film find is the nature of this essential, core masculinity? Schizoid breakdown and anarchist terrorism. Is *this* what a real man is, Tyler?

As ever, it is important to differentiate between representations of men in cultural contexts, especially those with strong commercial imperatives, and the daily realities of contemporary individuals. The only useful generalisation that can be made about the changes in masculinity is that there *is* no masculinity – instead there are many, many masculinit*ies*. In place of a solid answer to Tyler's question, there is now a very big question mark. Maleness is no longer (and probably never was) a fundamental lodestone that men could reach, hold and be empowered by. Some men may gleefully embrace the unabashed 'laddism' of *Zoo* magazine; millions of others do not. Media industries spend vast sums of money attempting to research and utilise such generalisations; when their marketing campaigns fail (though, increasingly, they are succeeding), they declare a 'crisis in masculinity', seemingly unaware that the only crisis is in trying to define what masculinity is.

What this guide will do is to look at the multiplicity of male roles, not just in terms of representation, but also by looking at films where directors both male and female have addressed the issues surrounding both traditional and modern male roles.

Why has there been such an increase in criticism about men and their roles, both socially and culturally? Why would it be valuable to study men and film?

Some answers lie in the impact of feminism. Though gender studies is now a popular topic – all the A Level specifications include topic areas that look at gender, so it is hard to avoid – the topic title is relatively recent. A university prospectus from the early 1980s would have listed the discipline under women's studies. Feminism had created a fervent interest in the way in which women had been oppressed by patriarchal society, and a questioning of what women's role in society really was; there was also a celebration of femininity and women's culture – female painters, writers, thinkers, filmmakers – that explored what it was to be a woman. However, what many men and women began to realise was that the insights feminism provided – about the way patriarchal society works – had just as much relevance to individual men's lives as individual women's. As Jeff Hearn (1987) stated: men oppress women, *and* other men. The questioning of women's traditional roles carries with it the flipside: the questioning of men's social roles; the insights (and contradictions) made by feminist thinkers also had profound implications for men. Women's studies was opened out into gender studies.

Men were, and still are, interested in what feminism revealed about women, and about themselves. If feminist women celebrated femininity and glorified in casting off the shackles of social convention and in disrupting the patriarchal hegemony, then surely couldn't men do something equivalent? That's where the myth of the 'crisis' originates: in exploring what it means to be a man in the swiftly changing modern world, men discovered that there were problems in celebrating masculinity – namely, which masculinity do you celebrate? The traditional male – the cowboy, the achiever, the breadwinner, the warrior? Feminism had exposed these as myths of a patriarchal society, unachievable images of strength and dynamism that 'real' individual men were imprisoned by, just as women have been imprisoned by their roles as mother, virgin or whore. So where was the 'new man'? In the bestselling and iconic 1980s Athena poster of the hunk gently cradling a baby? Or in history, the more primitive – but less complicated – traditional male: hunter, defender, tribesman?

Students today, again of both sexes, accept as a given the goals that 1960s' and 1970s' feminism strove to achieve. They have also, contrarily, been brought up with the Spice Girls claiming a victory for 'girl power' by wearing high heels and short skirts, a brand of feminism that the traditional feminist is likely to be appalled by. When students begin to approach gender studies, they are often surprised that the ideas discussed in the universities of their parents' generation are as valid and challenging today as they were then. They often take to the subject personally – after all, to young people, developing an identity is the most vital of projects, and gender is a huge part of who we are. Intelligent young men are just as interested in the social construction of gender as female students, and female students are often just as interested in the issues surrounding masculinity as they are femininity. While introducing feminism to students, I've noticed that as the discussion about representations of women or 'feminine' writing/filmmaking styles begins to evolve, we need to increasingly also discuss men and masculinity in order to balance the arguments. Students, their teachers and wider audiences are growing aware of these issues and many films explore them in insightful and relevant ways. This guide hopes to provide an introduction to these debates by using specific film texts and focus directors, while contextualising them with some critical perspectives on 'masculinist' issues, and on how feminist criticism raises questions about men as spectators.

How to use this guide

The first section outlines ideas on how to teach this topic, by using the focus films and directors from the case studies (in Section 3) to introduce issues and critical perspectives on the changing role of men and how these are explored in cinema. There are also ideas on how to organise an independent research project on the topic area.

The second section provides essential background and contextual information about the changes in masculinity over the past 30 years. It looks at the values and roles of traditional masculinity and femininity and attempts to place the changes to those values and roles in a social and historical context. This section also introduces different responses to changes in gender roles, and how these link to two alternate critical perspectives: postmodern and essentialist. There is also an introduction to Laura Mulvey's influential ideas about male spectatorship in cinema, and other theoretical responses to her notion of the 'male gaze'; there are, as well, some ideas about how to examine and debate so-called masculine and feminine filmmaking styles and their relationship to the mainstream cinema.

The third section contains case studies of specific films and directors who explicitly explore masculinity and address men's issues. It looks at how three films examine male roles in the world today:

- *Fight Club* (David Fincher, USA, 1999) – comments on the 'confusion' of men, and links to Robert Bly's ideas about the importance of pre-industrial, primitive ritual in men's lives.
- *The Return* (Andrei Zvyagintsev, Russia, 2003) – explores the role of the Oedipal father and mother in the life of the maturing boy, and the painful process of 'becoming a man'.

- *Y tu mamá también* (Alfonso Cuarón, Mexico, 2001) – explodes the *machismo* that is universal among adolescent males, and raises questions about Latin masculinity that have resonance in all cultures.

There are also case studies of two directors who have very different approaches to representing and exploring masculine identity. The first is Todd Haynes, who questions not only homosexual but also heterosexual masculinity by appropriating previous cultural forms, from the melodrama to glam rock. The second is Paul Verhoeven, whose films have often been accused of crassly exploiting the traditional male desire for watching sex and violence, but who then subverts and questions these desires.

Throughout Section 3, there are analyses of key scenes that link to tasks in the worksheets that are available at www.bfi.org.uk/tfms. To access the pages, enter username: **menfilm@bfi.org.uk** and password: **te2007me**. If you have any problems, please e-mail education.resources@bfi.org.uk. In the case studies of directors, there are summaries of their key films, ideas to focus classroom discussion and suggestions for research projects that could reference the films.

Approaches to teaching

● Introducing theory

Although there is considerable debate between A Level Media/Film Studies teachers about how much media theory to use with students, there is no doubt that it is useful for students to extend their own primary response to media texts by reference to relevant critical theory. The teacher's role is of great importance here, firstly, in making often complex theories accessible and secondly, in enabling their students to apply the theory in a meaningful way. If critical perspectives are linked to specific textual examples, then not only are they relatively easy to explain to students, but students themselves find the ideas relevant and enlightening. Ultimately, 'theory' is not the product of an intellectual elite that non-academics cannot access: it is simply a collection of ideas that some people have developed in order to explain trends in culture and society; these could be the views of an individual thinker, a whole school of thought, or an ideology that can only be recognised in hindsight.

A good confidence-building exercise for students is to take a fairly accessible view – the essentialist view of gender, for example – and build personal arguments for and against it. Once students realise how easy it is to pick holes in the argument, and can challenge the theory with examples they have found themselves, then theory becomes a space where ideas, no matter how wacky or challenging, can be played with. With this intellectual freedom comes far greater confidence in developing their own viewpoints, and a sense of personal engagement. Students should be made to feel that *they* are critics too, that their insights and conclusions are just as valid and can be as enlightening as those of established writers. When they investigate a theory doing primary research, they can gather genuine audience feedback that can be used to not only argue for or against a topic, but, sometimes, to amend a theory or help it evolve into something new. During this stage, they also find it very encouraging to know that they are actually being more rigorous than Mulvey, who didn't do any primary research at all to test her theories!

● Structuring independent research

Students do find theory far less intimidating if they are directly engaged in testing a theory's validity. By investigating a particular critical view by doing both primary and secondary research, students are viewing theory as an organic, living discourse, but they generate findings and conclusions that enable them to actively take part in that discourse.

● Developing a hypothesis: on **Worksheet 8**, there are a list of macro topics – 'big' questions about the relationship between men and film – that summarise some issues raised by different critical perspectives. Students should try to create a hypothesis that initially tries to answer two to three of these questions.

● Choosing focus films: once a hypothesis eg male spectators are unaware of voyeuristic desires being exploited in film – has been established, the student needs to make a list of texts to focus on. This should include one or two films that seem to prove the hypothesis, and some which could challenge it.

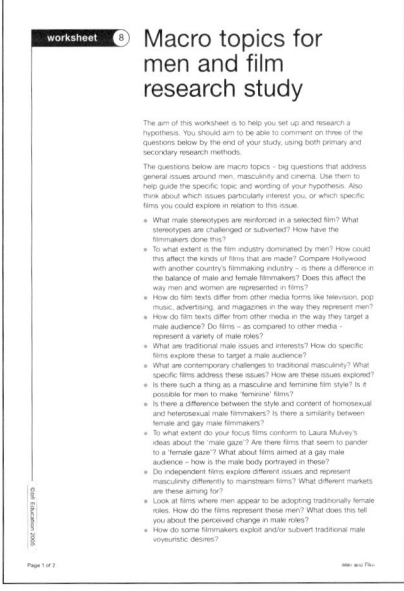

To access worksheets and other online materials go to **www.bfi.org.uk/tfms** and enter User name: **menfilm@bfi.org.uk** and Password: **te2007me**.

- Analysis: in order to get ideas for their methodology, students should do their own analysis of their chosen films, and see how their own reaction could support or challenge their hypothesis. They should then attempt to find one or more piece of criticism about these focus films – do the critics agree with the students' findings?

- Primary research: students could use a variety of methodologies to test audience reactions. In Section 3's director case studies there are summaries of key information about the films, then a number of questions that would give the student ideas for their methodology. In addition, students can also use the abundance of chatrooms and 'viewer review' pages for websites that sell films like Play.com and Amazon.

- Secondary research: often, once students have grasped the initial tenets of an idea, they can approach critical articles directly. They can recognise the ideas that they know, and can then begin to appreciate how this particular writer is challenging or developing that viewpoint. Encourage different reading strategies: highlighting key passages then attempting to paraphrase their ideas into students' own language, brainstorming findings in an attempt to link viewpoints together.

- Monitoring: although some specifications are very definite about research projects being a student's own independent work, this does not mean they can 'just get on with it' for five weeks. A good monitoring strategy is to have weekly 15- to 20-minute interviews with each student or small groups of students working on similar topics: they present what they have discovered over the past week and how they have achieved their targets. The teacher can then discuss the findings, assisting students in developing conclusions, and setting targets for the following week. These targets should attempt to develop the research, if possible beyond the confines of the initial hypothesis: films with a different ideology, by gay/straight, male/female, mainstream/non-mainstream directors, or from different cultures (and industries); a selection of test subjects with a different age, sex, class or cultural background.

- Extrapolation: when the time assigned to the project is drawing to a close, again refer to the list of macro topics. Ask students to look at each, then at their results. What can their specific findings (the 'micro' evidence) tell them about these topics? Ask students to make a list of five bullet points of 'macro comments' they can now make about the relationship between men and film and to provide one piece of specific evidence to support that comment.

● **Note on focus films**

The films and directors chosen for case studies are mostly intended for an adult audience, and nearly all of them have a 15 or 18 certificate in the UK. They do contain intense scenes of sex and violence, or have adult themes, but the study of masculinity and other gender issues does involve frank discussion of some sexual matters. It is advised that teachers think carefully about the sensitivity of their individual students; in some cases, it may be appropriate to use alternative texts to study the same issues. Having said that, if we bear in mind that in GCSE English *Lord of the Flies* (William Golding, 1954) and *The Color Purple* (Alice Walker, 1982) are options for set texts, and that some A Level specifications have *Enduring Love* (Ian McEwan, 2000), *The Handmaid's Tale* (Margaret Atwood, 1985) and *Oranges Are Not the Only Fruit* (Jeanette Winterson, 1985) as set texts, it can be argued that discussion of adult themes, using texts with adult content, is not just acceptable but a *requirement* in the education of young adults.

Schemes of work

The two schemes included can be divided into 'Explaining theory' and 'Applying theory'. Although designed to be used together, the first scheme of work would be a good introduction to gender for an examination of the relationship between women and film (OCR Critical Research Study), or for any topic about the representation of gender in the media (SQA Media Investigation).

Scheme of work 1 is designed for the beginning of A2 Level, although more able students in AS could use some of the material if analysing representations of gender, or where a more 'boy-centric' emphasis is needed when introducing notions of ideology and identity. Additionally, the analysis of men and women's roles in *Y tu mamá también* and *The Return* could be used to examine World cinema, and another culture's ideologies.

Scheme of work 2 is preparation for individual research projects where students will investigate a range of critical perspectives (Mulvey, postfeminist, Queer, masculinist, postmodern) and audience responses to specific films. The lessons that model research into the films of specific auteurs could also be used as stand-alone introductions to auteur theory.

● 1. Explaining theory: Introducing gender theory and ideas of masculinity

Aims:

To promote understanding of:

- Gender as a social construction
- Traditionally masculine traits
- The impact of feminism on men
- Male reactions to feminism
- Gay cinema, and the movement of gay culture into the mainstream

Outcomes:

Students will produce:

- Comparisons of texts aimed at male and female audiences
- Textual analysis of differing representations of masculinity
- Comparisons of 'straight' and 'gay' readings of mainstream films

Week 1 Introduction to gender theory

Introduce the idea that gender is a socially determined not biologically determined phenomenon

Identify traditional male and female values. Compare two adverts from children's TV, one aimed at boys, one at girls. What values are being targeted?

Are intrinsic male/female traits being appealed to? Or reinforced?

Worksheets 1 and 2

List traditional male and female traits. Find two characters from film/TV that have these traits. How are they represented? Find examples of characters who go against these traits

Worksheet 2

Look at David Gilmore's list of male social roles, and how they can be linked to traditional masculine traits and values. Choose some examples of male characters in films who fulfil these roles. Which characters do not? Look at the environment of each character – what influence does it have?

Worksheet 3

Week 2 Feminism and its impact

Explain the basic tenets of 'second-wave' feminism in the1960s. What influence might this have had on men?

Deconstruction of masculinity and men. *Y tu mamá también* – tenets of Latino/traditional masculinity taken apart by an independent woman; male fantasies exploded

Worksheet 18

Week 3 Reactions and responses to feminism
Crisis in masculinity? Or in how to market to men?
Mytho-poetic reaction – *Iron John*. Plus rise of 'male
fundamentalism' vs 'metrosexual' male
Analysis of *Fight Club*'s representation of the 'crisis' – attacking
'new men' but despairing of 'male tribalism'
Worksheet 10

Week 4 'Reconstructed' men and 'Queer' readings
Idea of 'reconstructed man' as secure in masculinity enough to
integrate traditionally feminine traits. Examples from magazines
Celebrating while criticising? Look at the films of Paul Verhoeven.
How do their plots and advertised content target traditional male
desires? Watch some scenes. How has voyeuristic desire been
subverted?
Introduce ideas of mainstream and alternative cultures. Examples
of marginalised gay culture vs 'acceptable' homosexuality
Introduce idea of heteroglossia – gay readings of mainstream films
Study gay reading of *The Lord of the Rings* at www.baywindows.
com/news/2002/12/12/Fun/A.Gay.Telling.Of.Lord.Of.The.Rings-
341243.shtml and attempt 'Queer' readings of a mainstream film
Gay auteurs – Todd Haynes and his portrayal of homosexuality
Analysis of *Far from Heaven* – postmodern exploration of
homosexuality

● **2. Applying theory: Masculinity in cinema**

Aims:
To promote understanding of:
● How men and women view men in films
● Feminist film theory and its views on men and film
● Ideas about the fetishisation of the male body
● How male and female audiences are targeted using differing
  representations of men
● Auteur theory and the work of directors who explore masculinity

Outcomes:
Students will produce:
● Research study into the likes/dislikes of male and female audience
  members of representations of men in films
● Exercises in trying to target male audiences
● Critical research study into men as audiences/spectators

Week 1   Audiences and men on film
What do students as individuals dislike/like about the way men are represented in film?
One week mini-research project – students choose a focus film and devise a questionnaire for both male and female audiences to investigate their reactions to an array of representations
Worksheet 5

Compare results and try to draw conclusions

Week 2   Laura Mulvey and the 'male' gaze
Introduce the ideas of John Berger with *Ways of Seeing* extract.
Introduce ideas about the 'male' gaze in cinema with summary of Mulvey's ideas (Mulvey's original article 'Narrative Pleasure …' is too difficult for most students)
Using trailer for *Charlie's Angels: Full Throttle* comment on how the characters are empowered, and how they are eroticised
Worksheet 4

Week 3   Eroticisation of men
Brainstorm retorts to Mulvey and examine the critical responses
Analyse 'Magic Man' scene with Josh Hartnett from *The Virgin Suicides*. Compare to fight scene/Brad Pitt in *Fight Club* – to what extent has the male body been eroticised?
Worksheet 6

Week 4   Targeting male audiences
Look at posters and trailer for *Y tu mamá también* – how is a male audience being attracted to a film that actually criticises traditional masculinity? Look at posters for *Fight Club* – how do these target both traditional and 'reconstructed' men?
Worksheet 18

Look at some synopses of some films that have been successful with male audiences – using results of questionnaires from Week 1
What values of different male 'types' are being targeted? What contemporary male 'issues' are being explored? Design a poster which would market one of these films. Compare to ad campaigns for an existing film with similar content/values

Week 5 Auteurs
Introduce idea of the auteur – a typically paternal role?
Auteurs who deal explicitly with nature of masculinity – students
research plots and audience reactions to four films by different
auteur directors. What male roles/issues are they exploring?
Worksheet 7

Week 6 Beginning a research project
Generating a hypothesis – using Todd Haynes and Paul Verhoeven
as auteurs to link to questions from 'macro topics'
Worksheet 8

Example: Todd Haynes. How is the traditional male deconstructed in
Far from Heaven? How is gender itself put under question in *Velvet
Goldmine*? Contrast masculine and feminine approaches to Julianne
Moore's condition in *Safe*
Students develop their own hypotheses, linking to 'macro topics'
Worksheet 9

Weeks 7–11
Monitoring of student research – primary results discussed, compared
to critical views and other researchers' findings
Extrapolation – how can specific 'micro' findings enable the students
to make comments about the 'macro' questions?

2

Background

This section will provide contexts – historical, cultural and theoretical – in which to place the case studies of specific films/directors, or any film a teacher or student may wish to focus on. It is divided into two main parts. The first will look at traditional gender roles, and offer some suggestions of historical events that may have triggered changes in the role of men and representations of masculinity. It also examines the work of two theorists – David Gilmore and R W Connell – who have explored the meaning of masculinity, and links these ideas with two cultural responses to changes. The second explains key critical perspectives that either examine masculinity and gender, or that are reactions to the changes documented in the first part. This links in with opening lessons of the Schemes of work in Section 1, and could be used in conjunction with the worksheets in introducing students to the issues surrounding men and cinema.

There is a moment in Hal Hartley's film *Trust* (USA, 1990), where a cynical woman challenges the hero about his attitudes. 'If you were a *real man*, you'd …' The hero slumps exhaustedly against the fridge and returns: 'God. I don't know if I could *stand* to be a real man.' His statement is an amusing retort, but also indicates something far deeper. To this character, being a 'real' man isn't about finding some kind of essence of true maleness within him. Instead, the phrasing gives the impression that this (traditionally) male role is nothing more than a lifestyle choice – a choice the hero finds distasteful, and which he is rejecting in much the same way as a rebellious youth may reject his parents' expectation that he settles down and gets a mortgage. In today's Western culture there are as many masculinities as there are femininities. The role of men in society has gone through a variety of significant changes since World War II, and each 'new' masculinity that arises becomes another valid role for actual men, and another role that is explored in cinema. But to appreciate the changes in what exactly a 'real man' is seen to be, we need to examine how the traditional gender roles defined men and women.

Traditional gender roles

Traditional gender roles are those that have become consensually constructed and largely accepted over time. Dr Robert Stoller was the first to explicitly separate biological sex and gender, but Ann Oakley (1972) expanded on the notion that gender is culturally determined. The following traditional gender values and traits are most evident in advertising, notably those aimed at children. Encourage your students (in conjunction with **Worksheet 2**) to record a few hours of teatime or Saturday morning children's programmes and analyse the adverts. Many of the following assumptions about boys' and girls' natures and specifically different traits are blatant and could introduce ways of identifying and defining traditional male and female roles. It doesn't get much more sophisticated when targeting adults! (For an excellent resource of over 2,000 print adverts that represent men and women in stereotypical ways go to www.genderads.com.)

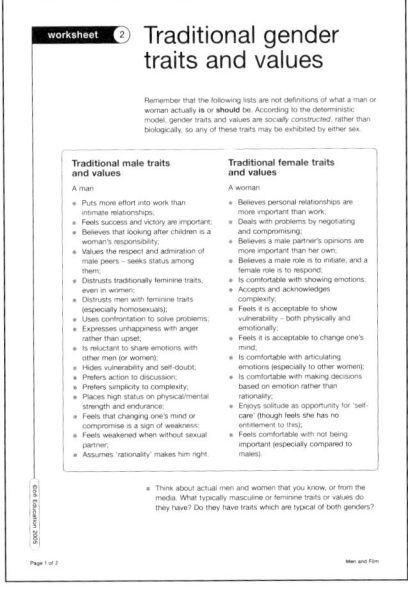

1 of 2 pages

To access worksheets and other online materials go to **www.bfi.org.uk/tfms** and enter User name: **menfilm@bfi.org.uk** and Password: **te2007me**.

● Traditional male traits and values

A man:

- Puts more effort into work than intimate relationships;
- Feels success and victory are important;
- Believes that looking after children is a woman's responsibility;
- Values the respect and admiration of male peers – seeks status among them;
- Distrusts traditionally feminine traits, even in women;
- Distrusts men with feminine traits (especially homosexuals);
- Uses confrontation to solve problems;
- Expresses unhappiness with anger rather than sadness;
- Is reluctant to share emotions with other men (or women);

- Hides vulnerability and self-doubt;
- Prefers action to discussion;
- Prefers simplicity to complexity;
- Places high status on physical/mental strength and endurance;
- Feels that changing one's mind or compromise is a sign of weakness;
- Feels weakened when without sexual partner;
- Assumes 'rationality' makes him right.

- **Traditional female traits and values**

A woman:
- Believes personal relationships are more important than work;
- Deals with problems by negotiating and compromising;
- Believes a male partner's opinions are more important than her own;
- Believes a male role is to initiate, and female role to respond;
- Comfortable with showing emotions;
- Accepts and acknowledges complexity;
- Feels it is acceptable to show vulnerability – both physically and emotionally;
- Feels it is acceptable to change one's mind;
- Is comfortable with articulating emotions (especially to other women);
- Sometimes makes decisions based on emotion rather than rationality;
- Enjoys solitude as opportunity for 'self-care' (though feels she has no entitlement to this);
- Feels comfortable with not being important (especially compared to males).

Just by thinking of actual men and women, we can see that these are now considered to be sexist stereotypes; yet their ubiquity in the media is startling when we look closely. The same values and behaviour have also been identified by sociologists examining masculinity in history and in other cultures, like Victor Seidler and David Gilmore.

If the modern man and woman are not confined by these anachronistic definitions, then changes in society and culture must have permitted the breaking down of these roles.

Historical background

To understand the changes that masculinity has undergone, it is first necessary to look at the fundamental changes in women's roles.

- **Pre-1940: The first wave of feminism**

Women had won the landmark right to vote for women (for over 21) in Britain in 1928. It would be a mistake to assume men opposed this, even if there was initial patriarchal resistance; there were Men's Federations for Women's Suffrage in both Britain and the USA. The right to vote, however, did not reflect women's growing empowerment. Ann Oakley (1974) noted that it was during the latter 19th and early 20th centuries that the association of men with the workplace and women with the home first emerged. Legislation like the Factory Acts first stopped children working (implying that there needed to be someone at home to look after them) and male-only trade unions led to women being excluded from the workplace.

● World War II: Start of first 'women's culture'?

As the majority of the men had been sent away to fight – as in World War I – women were encouraged to take up the jobs they had left behind; during the war years, women in factories, on farms, in dockyards, and in offices kept the economy running. During this time, they were also able to talk to each other outside the home, and recognise common experiences; some critics have said that this is where the feminist culture of the late 20th century began. For some young women, their first experience of adulthood meant taking on responsibility in a job, and when the men returned at the end of the war many didn't want to give up the independence they had grown used to. Barbara Ehrenreich (1983) isolates the female role in the economy as one of the principal reasons for the decline in patriarchal power in the latter half of the century; while host of Radio 4's Women's Hour, Jenni Murray, summarises the situation anecdotally: 'An old friend told me her first wage as a war worker acted on her like a drug, she couldn't give up her financial independence!' (2001)

● 1950s–60s: Second-wave feminism

During the social upheaval that followed World War II, the feminist cause was inextricably tied up with the birth of liberal culture. Closely allied to Civil Rights and anti-war demonstrations, feminism began to question the role of women, and the (male) power structures that defined them. Betty Friedan published *The Feminine Mystique* in 1963, its central thesis being that women had been encouraged to live vicariously through their husbands and children instead of gaining fulfilment from genuinely stimulating work. Friedan founded the National Organisation for Women in 1966, which called for significant legal changes to give women more power and autonomy. Other feminists began the task of both reclaiming historical images of women from the male viewpoint and attempting to establish a female perspective that more accurately reflected women's experience. In 1960, the birth control pill was introduced in Britain and America, for the first time giving women their own control over reproduction and facilitating the separation of sexual pleasure from procreation. This led to a repositioning of sexuality within society: if women weren't doing it purely for the perpetuation of the species, what were they doing it for? Fun? If so, then they better make sure it *is* fun! The search for sexual fulfilment (initially for women) became one of the key personal goals in Western society from this point on.

● Late 1970s: Feminism moves out of the academy and into popular culture

Friedan and Germaine Greer (with *The Female Eunuch* in 1970) had shown that books by women, about women's experiences, could be bestsellers, and in 1973, Carmen Callil started Virago, the first woman's publishing house. In 1972, Gloria Steinem founded *Ms.* magazine to explore women's issues. It seemed as if a serious change was occurring in the balance of power between men and women. The law reflected this more clearly than any book or magazine: after Steinem's 'pro-choice' activism, abortion was legalised in the US in 1973, while in the UK, the Equal Pay Act of 1970, and the Sexual Discrimination Act of 1975 formalised women's right to financial independence. It was as a reaction to this eruption of popular feminism that the stereotype of the man-hating feminist arose. Kate Millett published *Sexual Politics* in 1971, and was the first to use the term *patriarchy* to describe the male-dominated power structure, but as early as 1977 Sheila Rowbotham stated that individual men and boys were often victims of patriarchy, too. Men, however, in documentary interviews, and in TV sitcoms, soaps and movies, confessed to feeling under attack. Patriarchal society seemed responsible for every injustice, yet actual men felt they had done little themselves to oppress women. Not only did they feel under attack, but there were a new set of expectations was placed on them. It seemed, certainly in the pages of *Cosmopolitan* and modern girl's magazines, that women were empowering themselves with a new set of expectations of men: men who would be sensitive, who would take equal role in domestic responsibilities, who could provide satisfying sex and encourage a partner to pursue a successful career.

● Thatcherism and economic change

The 1980s' obsession with material success led to traditional masculine values – while still being dismantled by feminism – being adopted by some women themselves. The 'power-dressing' businesswoman that we can see in TV's *Dynasty*, revelled in her masculine traits and her equal status with, or even dominance over, men. Radical feminists like Barbara Ehrenreich (1995) later saw this as a kind of machismo, the same rejection and denial of the feminine and women's culture in order to celebrate brutish manliness. Ehrenreich said that one of the side effects of feminism and the struggle for equality was a decline in 'chivalric' masculinity: man as a provider and protector. She noted that men were becoming more comfortable with women taking an equal economic role in the domestic milieu, but this was also leading to women being expected to behave as men do in the workplace. If men were to take equality seriously, they expected women to adapt to a competitive, aggressive working style. In the opinion of many, this challenge to women was personified by the British Prime Minister Margaret Thatcher (1979–92): morally conservative (encouraging traditional 'family values' in the face of a soaring divorce rate) while economically liberal – encouraging *everyone* to work, to be as successful as they could be. It was also during this period that the Conservative government began to dismantle the traditional manufacturing industries (the male domain) and shift jobs to offices and ICT services. (*The Full Monty*, Peter Cattaneo, UK, 1997, would provide a good example of this.) Jonathan Rutherford (1988) identified widespread unemployment and the decline of manual heavy industry as key changes that had undermined male dominance; many men were now denied the role of 'breadwinner', and while this led to anxiety and frustration in many, some also began to question their role in the patriarchy and in wider society. Rutherford discussed how the anxious male ego created what he calls 'retributive men' who try to strongly reassert traditional masculine values. He links this image of masculinity to Thatcher-Reaganite politics – the tough, no-nonsense, no-compromise attitude to a world gone soft – and to cultural icons like Rambo, violently defending traditional concepts of honour. Other men, who Rutherford names 'new men', emerged, too, men who were aware of the damage wrought by patriarchy, and who were conscious of their own potentially damaging masculine drives. Emotional males, struggling with their feelings and the changes in society began to emerge in films of the period, too: movies like the sex comedies of Woody Allen and *Kramer vs Kramer* (Robert Brenton, USA, 1979), in which a father battles his wife for custody of their son, show a different side of 1980s' masculinity to the Stallone and Schwarzenegger warrior model.

● AIDS and the 'Queering' of the mainstream

One ironic side effect of the nature of the Thatcher–Reagan culture was the movement of gay culture towards the mainstream. There are two main causes for this. Firstly, the emerging AIDS pandemic, and the threat of it spreading through the heterosexual community, forced a neo-conservative West to deal explicitly and openly with mainstream and alternative sexualities. While forcing people to finally discuss 'the love that dare not speak its name', it also reinforced homophobic views of gay culture as dangerous, threatening and deviant. Nonetheless, homosexuality began to be accepted as an integral part of society – and, ironically, the capitalist boom, the second cause, aided this.

During the late 1980s, industry discovered the notion of the 'pink pound': many gay men occupied well-paid jobs, had no children and large disposable incomes, with their main outlay being lifestyle products. Although Thatcherite culture may have morally disapproved of homosexuality, the high status of the consumer in society meant that the *gay consumer* was encouraged. The popular media exploited this: TV, magazine, film and pop music actively targeted the gay audience (making lots of money), while liberals applauded the new tolerance such pop culture seemed to be announcing. In his book, *Masculinities*, R W Connell describes how this established homosexual culture was a genuine alternative to hegemonic masculinity; though gay theorist Jeffrey Weeks (1991) notes that it was during the 1980s that the image of the gay man as effeminate and unmanly began to be replaced by the 'machoised' gay body – strong, muscular, with an eroticised air of violent threat – and suggests that this both enabled heterosexual society to accept gay sexuality, but also made traditional male physical values problematic: if the pinnacle of manliness was now also the paragon of homosexual desire, then what should heterosexual men aspire towards?

● Impact on masculinity

These social and cultural influences led to a number of changes to the traditional male role:

- Women's economic independence meant that, in a capitalist society, there is now an economy – and a culture – based on women. In media terms, they are seen as men's equals.
- The national trend to dismantle heavy industry and move towards service and ICT industries has reduced the amount of traditionally male jobs. Legislation has also granted women the same career opportunities as men (if not always equal pay), as well as an equal education.
- In many families, the mother and father both work, meaning the economic power in the family relationship has changed. Indeed a significant number of men have become the main childcarer if their partner is the higher paid worker.
- The criticisms of feminism have laid bare the myths of masculinity: the role models (heroic soldiers, philandering Casanovas, domineering fathers) have been exposed as destructive myths. The society created by men has been attacked, and many men recognise that men are as oppressed by its power structure as women.
- The repositioning of gay culture into the mainstream has led to a tolerance towards homosexual men, especially among women. The positioning in *Will and Grace* (David Kohan and Max Mutchnick, USA, 1998) and *My Best Friend's Wedding* (P J Hogan, USA, 1997) of the gay man as 'woman's best friend' has encouraged men to 'get in touch with their feminine side' (Queer theorists would object to the definition of 'gay' as 'feminine').

- The attempt by the advertising industry to prematurely address this by announcing the 'new man' backfired with both men and women, leading to the late 1990s' 'new lad', as targeted by *Loaded* magazine – an attempt to balance the male ego with an awareness of the status of women in the modern world.

Timeline of masculinist thinking

Though there have been 'men's groups' that explore and challenge male behaviour and values since the 19th century (Sir Arthur Conan Doyle ran one in New York in the 1890s), a men's movement didn't really emerge until men began to respond to the challenges of feminism. In the 1970s, this reaction began to form into two different schools of thought. The first is what Warren Farrell (in *The Liberated Man*, 1974) termed the 'pro-feminist' which, as the name suggests, supported the views of feminists that men were responsible for the oppression of women, and suggested that men needed to do 'men's work' to explore where destructive masculine tendencies originated, and how to cope with them. The other school is the Male Liberationist or masculinist perspective, whose proponents (like Herb Goldberg and Richard Doyle) believe that men are victims, too, that the patriarchy and feminism have both 'wounded' male individuals who now have to work together to 'heal' each other (a viewpoint we can see lurking in the subtext of a film like *Fight Club*).

Sociologists didn't turn their attention to the issue of men and masculinity until the 1990s. But then many thinkers and writers like David Gilmore and Jonathan Rutherford began to examine what masculinity meant, looking at historical antecedents and comparing Western models to those of different cultures. Below is a timeline of writers' and critics' major works, and a summary of their ideas.

1968   Dr Robert Stoller first to separate sex from gender
1972   Ann Oakley publishes *Sex, Gender and Society* in which she argues that traditionally masculine and feminine traits are not defined by sex, but by culture. She describes the cultures of Mbuti pygmies in the Amazon, Aborigines in Tasmania, and the Communist states of China and the USSR where there is little difference in the working roles of men and women.
        John Berger publishes *Ways of Seeing* which analyses the way women are represented for the male gaze in Western art.
1974   Warren Farrell publishes *The Liberated Man*, arguing that men have to take responsibility for patriarchal oppression and work with feminists to expose masculine destructiveness. The book was considered to be the pro-feminist male manifesto.

1976   Herb Goldberg publishes *The Hazards of Being Male* which first outlines the masculinist perspective, suggesting that men too are oppressed by the patriarchy and that much male rage comes from the frustration of being unable to fulfil traditional expectations.

Richard Doyle, a leading figure in the campaign for men's legal rights, publishes *The Rape of the Male*, which supports the socio-biological view of male and female traits, arguing that men cannot help being the way they are, and that their work involves reconciling core masculine traits with a changing society.

1978   Men's Awareness Network founded to support pro-feminist men.

1979   David Barash applies socio-biology to gender roles, explaining that gender traits have developed because men and women have learnt behaviour to ensure they reproduce efficiently.

Richard Haddard publishes *Manifesto for the Men's Liberation Movement*, which rejects socio-biology and insists gender roles and masculinity are culturally encouraged. This arouses the ire of feminists because it also states that women should take some responsibility for perpetuating both male and female stereotypes.

1988   Jonathan Rutherford publishes *Male Order: Unwrapping Masculinity* in which he documents some of the changes in masculinity, and isolates the challenges Western males face from the changes to social and economic structures. Rutherford said that white heterosexual men have historically feared women, homosexuals and Black men – and that part of the 'crisis' in masculinity has been caused by these three groups achieving a very vocal empowerment in the 1960s–80s.

1990   David Gilmore publishes *Manhood in the Making: Cultural Concepts of Masculinity*.

1992   Robert Bly's *Iron John* stresses a spiritual instead of political approach to the problems of men in society (see page 34).

1993   In *Backlash*, Susan Faludi proposes that there has been a 'masculinisation' of culture, where both men and women are rejecting many of the radical feminist ideas. This, Faludi suggests, is a result of men trying to win back some of the power they believed women claimed in the earlier decades, and of women struggling to fit into an 'equal' (but persistently patriarchal) society.

1995   R W Connell publishes *Masculinities*, examining historical models of what he terms 'hegemonic masculinity', and, through many in-depth interviews, those models at the end of the 20th century.

In his essay, 'What's a Straight White Man to Do?' George Yudice becomes one of the first male writers to attack the men's movement for creating the myth of the victimisation of men.

1997   Victor Seidler, in *Man Enough: Embodying Masculinities*, attempts to locate the Western historical origins of traditional masculine traits. He argues that male values of rationality, the drive to control nature, and the suspicion of emotion originate in the Enlightenment and form the basis of 20th-century masculinity.

Two theorists, two cultural responses to changes in masculinity

• David Gilmore

Gilmore attempted to appease both deterministic ideas about gender (that masculinity was an entirely social construct) and the socio-biological view. He acknowledged that in many cultures there were three main roles for the male, which could explain traditionally masculine values: man the impregnator (sexual potency and fertility is valued); man the provider (wealth or being the breadwinner is valued – links also to career success); and man the protector (strength, aggression, physical endurance and territoriality is valued).

However, Gilmore goes on to look at a number of cultures, such as the Tahitian and the Semai, where men do not behave in this way. He says this indicates that the social and cultural context affects how an individual male uses or exaggerates his biological potential. In Tahiti, families live very close together and have to get along (which prevents excessive territoriality); there is a lagoon with plentiful stocks of fish, so there is no danger from hunting (therefore putting oneself at physical risk is neither necessary nor respected); and there is no history of war (physical strength and aggression are not necessary to protect the community). Gilmore concluded that the masculine values a culture developed were strongly influenced by the needs imposed by the environment – if there was no actual need to develop traditionally male traits, then cultures tended not to.

• R W Connell

Connell in *Masculinities* also believes that there are many different types of masculinity in society; he looks at the historical precedents for this, then compares them to a number of empirical studies of Australian men. Connell looks at different historical periods and the varieties of male roles, and he notes that there is always a 'hegemonic masculinity' – that is, a dominant model, which is then interpreted or resisted by individual men. This is by no means stable and static, and Connell traces how it has developed from feudalistic society to the present day, linking the particular values to the demands of the society at the time (agreeing with Gilmore). He says that late 20th-century men are affected by two big influences.

Firstly, in what Connell calls 'metropolitan' countries, feminist critiques, the rise of demands for racial equality and the movement of homosexuality to the mainstream offer a range of male values alternative to the dominant forms. Simultaneously, though, globalisation has taken the most aggressive and capitalist male stereotypes and spread them across the world, so that every culture now has associations that link men with 'fast cars and powerful trucks' (Connell, 1995).

Studying interviews conducted with men from a range of class backgrounds, Connell found four main types of men that he said reflected the complexity of masculine roles in society today. The first came from principally working-class backgrounds, and seemed like examples of stereotypical Australian machismo: they regularly got into fights, treated women as sexual objects, and hated gay men. Connell calls this 'protest masculinity': bourgeois liberal society has not provided them with the economic means of attracting women and impressing men through material wealth, so they over-compensate with exaggerated displays of toughness.

However, when Connell questioned further, he found that many of these men had been brought up by a single mother; they had no problem with a woman being their economic equal and some even considered themselves 'feminists' who treated the women they knew badly because these women acted like stereotypically weak females. The second group were men of a similar 17 to 29 age bracket and a similar working-class background. They had all initially developed a macho set of values, but later had revoked these, mainly through their involvement with the environmental movement.

Through their experience with Green groups, where competition and territoriality were not encouraged, these men reassessed and changed their ideas about what manliness meant. A third group were what Connell termed 'very straight gays'. These were homosexual men who rejected the effeminacy stereotypically associated with gay culture, and who instead valued traditional masculine values both in terms of personal aspiration and in what they desired in other men. A fourth group were 'men of reason': males aged 20 to 40 who embodied many postwar male values such as rationality, being the breadwinner and a distrust of homosexuals – but who in no way associated this with physical strength or violence. Connell was quick to state that these were not static types, and that every individual had his own complex relationship with his own masculinity, other men, women and wider society.

● The metrosexual

The term was first used by Mark Simpson in his Salon.com article (2002), where he isolated a breed of urban professional males who took pleasure in their own appearance, without feeling any less masculine. Though there were men who indulged in conspicuous consumerism and took pleasure in their own image in the 1980s (as satirised by Bret Easton Ellis in *American Psycho*, 1991), the metrosexual also has an implied comfort with gay culture and a generally more emotional approach to situations. He is a man who has balanced his manliness and his 'feminine side'.

In June 2003, Euro RSCG Worldwide, a powerful marketing communications agency, explored the changing face of American males in a report titled 'The Future of Men: USA'. Men between the ages 21 and 48 throughout the USA were surveyed on masculinity-related issues. According to the report, there is 'an emerging wave of men who chafe against the restrictions' of traditional male roles and who 'do what they want, buy what they want, enjoy what they want – regardless of whether some people might consider these things unmanly'.

As with the move of gay culture into the mainstream during the late 1980s and 90s, anything that involves men – a notoriously difficult target market – confidently buying products is fully supported by popular culture. Even 'lads' mags' like *Maxim* and *FHM* – where the reader's assumed heterosexuality is overstated and reinforced by nearly naked female cover stars – have as many fashion and grooming pages as features on gadgets and strippers. As stated above, there is an acceptance of gay culture in most large cities – in fact, having a vibrant gay scene has become a selling point of many European tourist agencies – and *Friends*, a show with openly gay characters, is shown as part of Channel 4's breakfast TV schedule.

This shift by culture towards the mainstream has also shown heterosexual men that some 'gay' qualities are seen by women to be attractive – Johnny Depp and David Beckham are two media figures who are represented as being openly 'in touch with their feminine side', yet are regarded by women's magazine polls to be the sexiest men in the world. This male 'type' could be linked to both Connell's and Gilmore's ideas about the role of the environment – economic, geographic and cultural – in defining what is classed as masculine.

● Male fundamentalism

Anthony Giddens noted, in a 1994 ICA lecture on love and relationships, that because of the breakdown of traditional masculinity and the confusing array of expectations now placed on men, many men were opting for a kind of 'male fundamentalism': rejecting the complexities of the male ego that feminism and psychoanalysis had thrown up, opting for a simple, essentialist view of masculinity. Men are men – that's all there is to it; strip away the metrosexual's hair gel and Prada suit, remove the comfortable trappings of modern consumer culture, and there is a core essence of masculinity that defines men.

This reaction can be traced through religious fundamentalism, with its emphasis on male power and female 'modesty' (ie subordination) and through more 'New Age' initiatives like the men's drumming circles of California.

Robert Bly and Sam Keen (see page 34) are two authors who idealise the pre-industrial male roles (one of fellow 'masculinist' Robert Moore's books is even titled *King, Warrior, Magician, Lover*!) as being the 'real' essence of masculinity. R W Connell termed this 'protest masculinity', typical among men who feel like the modern culture of supposed gender equality has betrayed them: working-class men who cannot afford the trappings of the metrosexual, men who have been legally emasculated by divorce proceedings and custody battles. More critical writers like Susan Faludi and George Yudice have described this reaction as more of a 'temper tantrum' because men are confused about whether to hold a door open for a woman or not. What is significant is that this backlash against the 'feminised' 'new man' of the 1980s is becoming a potent force in marketing, as the success of the new 'lads' weeklies' like *Nuts* and *Zoo* indicate.

Theoretical context

● Postmodernism and identity

Although a full explanation of postmodernism ideally also needs to fully explain the tenets of modernism, it is possible to look specifically at how the ideas of postmodern thinkers explain the changes in identity and gender identity.

Key ideas:

- If there is no 'truth' then there is no 'true' identity, no 'real you' beneath the various socially accumulated layers. Jean Baudrillard, Michel Foucault and more recently Kenneth Gergen have commented on this erosion of 'core' identity.
- If there is no solid identity, this means that we are playing a series of roles. Our sexual and gender identities are not who we intrinsically 'are'; they are roles we play in different situations. Judith Butler talks about gender as a performance in her influential book *Gender Trouble* (1990):

  > There is no gender identity behind the expressions of gender; ... identity is performatively constituted by the very "expressions" that are said to be its results.

- Camille Paglia: 'Postmodernism is shopping'. What does she mean? Simply that in postmodernity, there is no stable, fixed identity, and that late capitalism has created a world where we are used to making choices about what we buy, and what it says about us. When we 'shop' in the postmodern world, we are surveying the array of personal choices on offer (like we would products in a shop) and selecting whichever take our fancy at that moment. Our identities are composites: ideas, beliefs, desires, hopes/fears, as well as superficial style, are sampled when convenient.

- How does this affect masculinity? Postmodernism goes against essentialist beliefs about gender. 'Men are men' is a useless tautology – instead, men are able to look at an array of masculine traits and roles, which they can choose to inhabit or reject, depending on their situation. A good example would be the comedian Eddie Izzard, a heterosexual man, who is proud of his masculinity, but who enjoys wearing make-up and 'women's' clothes. Izzard isn't gay and isn't a transsexual, but, almost sending up social labels, calls himself an action transvestite. He samples both masculine and feminine fashion codes (often combining a goatee beard with knee-length leather boots and lipstick) to fit how he feels.
- Postmodernism implies gender roles are there to be 'played' with. Traditional gender traits are not insightful observations into the way 'real' men and women behave – they are merely culturally accepted ideas which, like everything in culture, can be sampled, mixed and matched with other traits to build a temporary 'identity'.

Further reading: Postmodernism is a notoriously difficult concept. A good starting point is to ask students to research and summarise the main ideas of: Michel Foucault, Jean-François Lyotard, Jean Baudrillard, Camille Paglia, Judith Butler and Anthony Giddens. A good start would be the www.theory.org website. Another very good introduction, and a specific discussion of postmodernism and gender, is *Media, Gender and Identity: An Introduction* by David Gauntlett (2002).

Link to case studies:

- Read the summary of Judith Butler's ideas at www.theory.org.uk/ctr-butl.htm. What does Butler say about the way in which gender is developed and defined? How can we see this view of masculinity (/ies) promoted in *Velvet Goldmine* (UK/USA, 1998) and other Todd Haynes' films?
- How are the struggles of men to fit into established male roles – often established by 'male' genres in cinema like the war movie, Western, or science fiction – explored in Paul Verhoeven's films?
- Compare the two directors. How far could it be said that Haynes represents postmodern masculine identity as a liberating concept, whereas Verhoeven portrays it as a cause of anxiety?

● 'Mytho-poetic' masculinity

Robert Bly's influential book *Iron John* (1992), along with Sam Keen's *The Fire in the Belly* (1992) took a nascent 'men's movement' that had been building since the 1980s and made it a point of national discussion. Through the exploration of a Grimm Brothers' fairytale, Bly attempts to explain the problems that men face today: frustration, lack of a firm role, and violence towards men, women and society generally. He takes an essentialist view that men and women have intrinsic traits and drives that cannot be subsumed or repressed because current society doesn't accept them.

The main points he makes are:

● Men had clearly defined roles in pre-industrial society. They were required to be violent when hunting animals, and – when society became agriculturally based – to protect the farm and family against raiders. Modern society refuses men this role – unless required in wartime. This, Bly would say, is why men are traditionally attracted to explicitly violent content in films and to an aggressive, fast-paced visual style; perhaps action and war films enable male audiences to identify with this primitive role, and express their violent urges.

● Additionally, men in pre-industrial society had a much more active role in nurturing the male child. Because the family often worked and certainly ate together, a male child would be nurtured through infancy by its mother, then – as in 'primitive' cultures – would be trained by other men to be 'a man' (and why that was different to being a woman).

● As they approached adolescence and sexual maturity, boys were expected to go through a ritualistic test of their endurance, strength and self-reliance.

● In the last 200 years, this has changed. Men were expected to go to work, leaving mothers to bring up the sons until they too were at a working age. Not only have men been removed from the nurturing process – so that boys have no clear male role model – but they are not allowed to express the frustration and confusion they feel.

● The physical test in the rite of passage has now been subsumed into masochistic group behaviour like binge-drinking, or excessive drug use: the man who can endure the intoxication and the pain of the ensuing hangover/comedown has proved himself.

● Bly said that men today have two major problems with 'shame': they are embarrassed that they can no longer fulfil their 'hunter/gatherer' role, and the feminist explosion has passed guilt on to them for the history of female subjugation. The 'natural' way for men to express this shame is through anger; and society offers men no acceptable outlet to express this.

● He goes on to say that 'men's groups' are a safe, masculine place outside modern civilisation where men can express their turbulent emotions. They can express feelings in poetry, re-establish their 'male rhythm' in drumming circles, express their rage safely by beating the earth with their hands or a stick. Here men are 'reconnecting' with their 'natural' male state, with each other (without homophobia) and with themselves.

Link to case studies:

Encourage students to:

- Read the accessible Shepherd Bliss article introducing the 'mytho-poetic' men's movement at www.context.org/ ICLIB/IC16/Bliss.htm.
- Spot what elements of Bly's ideas about men's needs and frustrations in society are explored in *Fight Club*.
- Look at the behaviour of the father in *The Return*. To what extent could his brutish actions be justified as that of a role model, teaching his sons how to survive in the world? Note how the tender protectiveness of the mother is linked to Ivan's initial inability to jump off the tower but the sadistic provocation of the father enables him to conquer his fear.

● Feminist film theory and 'the gaze'

Although more obviously linked to portrayals of women in cinema, feminist film theory is relevant here for its (somewhat simplistic) ideas about the male spectator and their responses to action on the screen. Furthermore, as many critics have pointed out, ideas about the audience's 'desiring gaze' and the way film representations cater to this are as applicable to portrayals of men as women.

- The main ideas come from Laura Mulvey's 'Visual Pleasure and Narrative Cinema' (1975) but are preceded by John Berger's *Ways of Seeing* (1972). In this book (and accompanying BBC TV series), Berger examines the way power and 'looking' are related. He says that, from the Renaissance onwards, the visual arts started to become more and more realistic. From the 18th century on, many paintings were commissioned by private patrons to depict the extent of their material wealth. Frequently, women were included in these paintings – visually equated with the 'property' that surrounds them.
- Berger also points out the nudity and passive posture of these female subjects. The male viewer is attracted to the eroticised, passive female form; meanwhile, the phrasing of women as 'property' gives the male viewer a sense of ownership over the subject. The portrayal of women assumes there is a male, desiring viewer and it encourages that desire.
- The context for the viewing of these paintings is also important: usually paintings in this style were exhibited in the 'men only' environs of the drawing room. This means the subject and style was intended for the male spectator, among other males.

- Mulvey takes up this idea, finds psychoanalytic explanations for this activity and applies it to women and cinema. Her basic assumption is that in classical film narratives 'Men act; women are looked at' (1975). The active protagonist is male, while women's role seems to be little more than a 'prize'. We can see this in the James Bond subgenre, even the more recent films – Bond's first action in undermining the super-villain is to seduce the villain's lover; on discovery that his 'prize' has been stolen and sullied, the villain's response is to kill the woman, and erase the shame of being sexually outperformed by 007.

- Female characters, Mulvey asserts, are presented in such a way as to evoke voyeuristic pleasure in the male audience. Their passive behaviour denies them proper human status and the way the camera films their bodies makes them into little more than objects that the spectator 'owns' through their watching.

- According to the father of psychoanalysis, Sigmund Freud, the male's principal fear is that of castration. According to Mulvey (after Lacan), he is drawn to cinema because there his 'insecure sexual ego' can be edified. By identifying with the active, powerful male character and by feeling ownership of the passive female, the male spectator's ego is reinforced.

- In films with an active and strong female character, Mulvey says the woman is 'fetishised' – ie the source of fear or threat is transformed into a source of pleasure. In films, the strong woman is invariably also very beautiful, with long hair, a slim waist and long legs which are shown off at every opportunity, eg *Lara Croft: Tomb Raider* (Simon West, UK/Germany/USA/Japan, 2001)*; Charlie's Angels* (McG, USA/Germany, 2000). This prevents the 'insecure male ego' being scared of the strong woman (as the bearer of phallic power or phallic woman), and reasserts the idea that as long as strong women can be sexually 'owned' through the gaze, they are no threat.

- Mulvey wrote this seminal article in 1975, and since then cinema and society have changed significantly. Mulvey herself added comments on the female spectator in her article, 'Afterthoughts' (1981), but even then she doesn't identify what the 'female gaze' might be, or how women may eroticise men. Recent critics like Theresa De Lauritis and D N Rodowick have updated Mulvey's ideas to take into account the gay male viewer (who would have no real interest in objectified women!) and the many examples of the male body being fetishised for a *female* audience. The 'desiring' gaze, therefore, is not necessarily tied to the male spectator and nor are women the gaze's only source of pleasure.

Activities:

- Show the students the trailer for *Charlie's Angels: Full Throttle* at www.sonypictures.com/homevideo/charliesangelsfullthrottle/index.html. Look at behaviour, costume, camera movement/angle. In what ways are the Angels empowered (portrayed as efficient, clever, brave, strong, skilful etc)? In what ways are they fetishised/eroticised? **Worksheet 4**

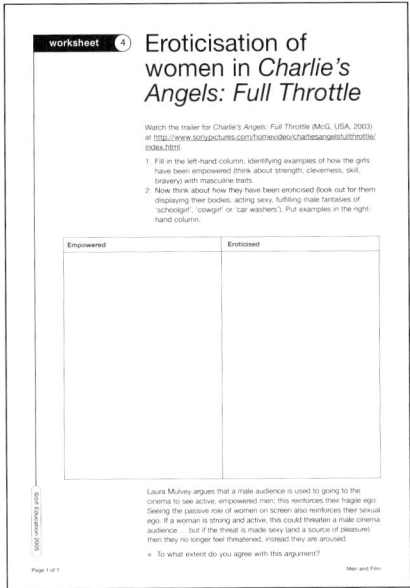

● Watch the scene near the beginning of *Rear Window* (Alfred Hitchcock, USA, 1954) where Jefferies is called by his agent who thinks that this is the day when the cast on his leg is removed. How is frustration in achieving traditional male goals (career success, action not discussion) redirected into voyeuristic pleasure? Another film, heavily influenced by Hitchcock, but going further in its obvious voyeurism is Brian De Palma's *Body Double* (USA, 1984). How is far is it assumed that the audience will be male, in the way we are asked to identify with the hero's point of view and in the portrayal of the women in the film?

● Watch the scene where Trip Fontaine (Josh Hartnett) is introduced in *The Virgin Suicides* (Sofia Coppola, USA, 1999). How is he eroticised? (Look at the way other female spectators in the film watch him, his poise and costume, camera movement, taking pleasure in his own appearance etc) **Worksheet 6**

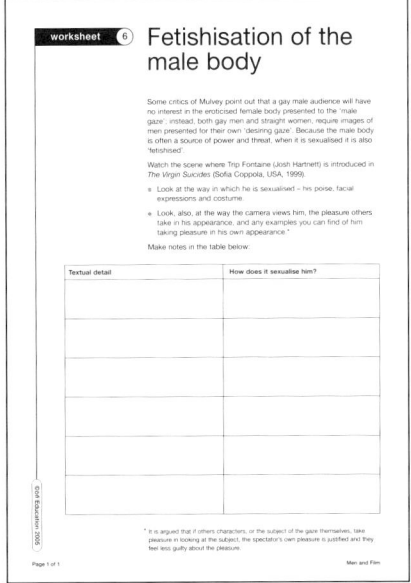

- Mulvey's ideas would also form a good basis for a research project into what male audiences like in films. Look at the films of Paul Verhoeven, who seems to exploit male desires and pander to the 'male gaze' but actually exposes it (see the analysis of the interrogation scene in *Basic Instinct*, USA, Verhoeven, 1992 – especially Tremmell 'returning' the desiring male gaze). **Worksheet 19**

To access worksheets and other online materials go to **www.bfi.org.uk/tfms** and enter User name: **menfilm@bfi.org.uk** and Password: **te2007me**.

worksheet 19 *Basic Instinct*: Supporting and subverting Mulvey's theories

Watch *Basic Instinct* (Paul Verhoeven, USA, 1992) from when Nick arrives to pick up Catherine, to the end of the interrogation scene, when she takes the lie-detector test.
Look at the textual details listed below.

- In the middle column identify which of these supports Mulvey's ideas about the male gaze and spectatorship. Explain how, briefly.

Now watch the scene again – thinking about how it appears to support Mulvey, but actually does something different. The woman is usually the passive receiver of the gaze; the men are the active characters – identifying with this dominant role strengthens the male spectator's sexual ego.

- The scene begins in this way, but how does the director use the female character and the camera to subvert Mulvey's ideas? Explain in the right-hand column.

Textual detail	Supports Mulvey	Subverts Mulvey
Nick glimpses Catherine naked as she slips into her dress (his POV).		
The men look Catherine up and down as she comes into the interrogation room.		
Catherine is seated on a lit stage, while the men surround her, in shadows.		
Catherine's dress is very short, emphasising her long legs – camera positioned at height of detectives.		
The detectives ask her probing questions about her sex life.		
Catherine answers them in detail.		

Page 1 of 1   Men and Film

1 of 2 pages

● Masculine/feminine or mainstream/alternative film style?

A debate that can lend focus to some of the issues raised by Mulvey and other feminist film theorists and filmmakers is whether male and female directors have intrinsically gender-based differences in the kind of films they make. Do films by female directors appeal more directly to a female audience, both in subject matter and style? Can male filmmakers explore female issues and direct in a 'feminine style'? What are masculine and feminine film styles anyway?

Ideas about what might be a masculine and feminine artistic style can be seen in art through the ages. Camille Paglia and others have discussed the origins of our cultural definitions of gendered art. Early religions based the gender of their gods (it is thought) on their own sexuality. So:

- Because men have the penis – genitals that are obvious, visible, exposed, and pointing forward – the Sun God was male. This is because the sun gives light, light we can *see* – so later, disciplines like science and maths are deemed as masculine because they seek to interpret and expose 'the truth'.
- Because women have the vagina – genitals that are hidden, out of sight, and internal – the main female deity was the Moon God. The moon is round like the womb, night is dark so things are hidden, secretive, mysterious. Imaginative/creative disciplines have been traditionally 'feminine' because they are on 'the inside', as are emotions. Plus, the effect of the moon on tides associates femininity with 'fluidity', cycles and smooth changeability.

From this ancient basis, our cultures have developed complex associations with masculinity and femininity. Feminist literary theorists like Hélène Cixous have discussed the difference in gendered writing: male literature tends to be narrative driven, linear (because this is how men experience sex: start, middle, end/climax) and full of visual description. Female writing tends to be character or stylistically driven, non-linear (because the female sexual experience can involve no climaxes or multiple spontaneous orgasms), with an emphasis on other senses, and on emotional responses.

Traits of 'masculine' cinema

- Lots of medium and long-distance shots so the subject and environment is fully visible. Visual spectacle is important.
- Fast, aggressive editing pace.
- Women's bodies provided for male gaze; camera responds to predictable male desires.
- Linear plot based around actions and behaviour.
- 'Objective' and 'realistic' use of *mise en scène* and camerawork; mechanics of film production hidden.
- Active male characters; traditional male traits and values are celebrated by narrative.

Traits of 'feminine' cinema

- The male gaze, and the way it defines/objectifies women is acknowledged and criticised.
- The male gaze is returned. The woman on screen seems aware that she is being viewed (compromising the voyeuristic thrill) and deliberately 'stares' back, forcing the viewer to take responsibility for the gaze.
- Narrative structure is non-linear and elliptical. There are gaps, hidden areas in the story that reflect femininity as 'secret' and 'mysterious'. Time may appear to speed up or slow down (feminine time is seen as fluid and subjective, not rigidly measured in hours/days).
- The camera's view is self-consciously subjective and emotional. The style is expressionistic: coloured tints, unusual angles/movement, fantastical/animated sequences; lighting, music, close-ups reflect characters' inner states. A different 'view' of reality is given.

These definitions are obviously flawed. If we look at filmmakers like Nora Ephron (*Sleepless in Seattle*, USA, 1993; *You've Got Mail*, USA, 1998) we can see that her visual style is far from the experimental, 'feminine' style of Lynne Ramsay (*Ratcatcher*, UK, 1999; *Morvern Callar*, 2002), not least because of their different institutional contexts, Hollywood mainstream cinema on the one hand and British independent cinema on the other. And, if we look at the career of the American actor and director Ida Lupino (which spanned the period 1933 to 1951) – who was also the most prolific film and TV director of either sex – her work was mainly in the male genres of cop and Western dramas. The US film director, Kathryn Bigelow, has resolutely rejected any notions of gendered direction and works almost exclusively in the 'male' genres of crime thriller and action-adventure. Then, if we turn to European filmmakers like Krzysztof Kieslowski in *The Double Life of Véronique* (France/Poland, 1991) and *Three Colours: Blue* (France/Poland, 1993), or Jean-Pierre Jeunet's *Amelie* (France, 2001), we can see a male director not only expressionistically representing the emotional state of his female characters but also using elliptical narrative and other so-called 'female' cinematic traits. Can we say then, that male and female directors make masculine and feminine films respectively? Is it more complex, or is the notion of 'gendered' cinema itself a red herring?

Perhaps it may be more accurate to discuss mainstream and alternative filmmaking styles, instead of trying to gender a particular film or style. If we think about the traits of 'masculine' cinematic style above, these are also the traits of mainstream Hollywood film. Look at the 'feminine' style and it fits a number of independent and 'arthouse' directors regardless of their sex. Can these differences be linked to gender at all then? Feminist film critics would argue that it can. Western society is both patriarchal and phallocentric. This means that those who own the means of film production, and those who have the money to spend on going to see films, are predominantly men. This may explain the dominance of male writers and directors in mainstream film production. Additionally, because our culture is phallocentric, this means the style and content of most films is designed to please male desires. Those whose content and film style go against the mainstream are therefore 'feminine' whether made by a woman or not.

A way for students to develop this debate further, and to practise primary research skills, would be to ask male and female audiences what they *like* to see in films. Can 'masculine' and 'feminine' film be defined not by the sex of the maker, but by the audience who enjoys it? This is a different approach to the debate, and one which could have interesting outcomes if students looked at reactions to the marketing, content and style of focus films like *K-19: The Widowmaker* (all-male cast in wartime submarine drama, directed by Kathryn Bigelow, USA, 2002) and *The Hours* (the life and struggles of women for independence over the years, directed by Stephen Daldry, UK/USA, 2002).

3

Case studies

Introduction

This section contains five case studies. The first three focus on individual films and select specific scenes for analysis and discussion. Case studies 4 and 5 examine the careers of two directors who explore contemporary masculinity in alternative ways. Their films are discussed, but there are also some ideas about how the directors build relationships with the audience. I have tried to select recent films that were either popular or critically acclaimed, but also tried to balance accessible, entertaining films with those that some students may find challenging. Although there are plenty of examples of both traditional male roles and the problems they face in classic Hollywood films, the films and directors I have selected represent not only very contemporary concerns about male identity, but also refer back to traditional roles in 'male' genres. There are worksheets that link to the specific scenes and, for the director case studies, there are suggestions for issues that students could investigate as part of research projects as well as ideas on how to expand the study of these themes by comparing the focus texts to other film/director examples.

Case study 1: *Fight Club* and male fundamentalism

David Fincher's film *Fight Club* is a good focus text for considering contemporary issues in masculinity for a number of reasons:

- It reflects many men's distaste at the 'feminisation' of men: mainly through the 'womanly' obsession with consumerist wealth which has replaced strength, honour and independence as male status symbols.
- It shows the rejection of a confused/open masculinity in favour of 'mytho-poetic' essentialism and, how out of this attitude, it is possible for fascism to be born.

● It explores the phenomenon of delayed adolescence: the weaker character bonding with the stronger, cooler, irreverent 'best mate'; ritualistic violence as a rite of passage; and the Oedipal relationship built with the mentor/father.

● Confused masculinity

Both Chuck Palahniuk, the author of the novel on which the film is based, and David Fincher, the director, have said that the story of *Fight Club* reflects and explores real men's lives today. Palahniuk said that he wrote his book 'in public', by talking to real men in diners, bars, coffee shops and their work places. He spoke to them 'about how they felt – and what they did to make themselves better' (Smith, 1999). Fincher said that the unnamed narrator of *Fight Club* is 'an everyman. Every young man.' In the film, there are three principal examples of the modern man's confusion over masculine roles and what being a 'man' actually means. Use **Worksheet 10** to focus students on the issues.

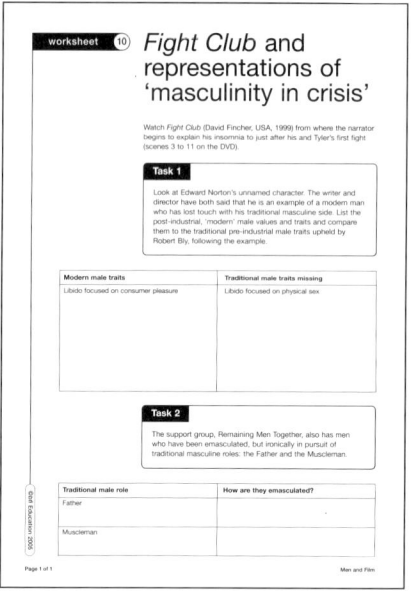

To access worksheets and other online materials go to **www.bfi.org.uk/tfms** and enter User name: **menfilm@bfi.org.uk** and Password: **te2007me**.

The first is the pre-*Fight Club* life of the narrator (played by Edward Norton – the fact that he is unnamed signals his lack of identity). He has achieved everything he has been told by his parents – and society – that he should achieve:

> He's been told, 'If you do this, get an education, get a good job, be responsible, present yourself in a certain way, your furniture and your car and your clothes, you'll find happiness.' And he hasn't. (Smith, 1999)

The male status he has achieved is an illusion, based on materialist accumulation and career hierarchy. He is in limbo. The pursuit of these false goals has subsumed his more 'naturally' male needs: he has no male friends, no sexual partner in the 'nest' apartment he's built, no physically demanding work or action-based solution to problems. His doctor tells him to get more exercise, and his libido has evaporated ('We used to read pornography; now we read the Ikea catalogue'). His method of actualising himself is through meaningless possessions – 'a refrigerator full of designer condiments and no food'- rather than corporeal action, and it is a method which his mentor, Tyler Durden, later deems irrelevant in an essential 'hunter/gatherer sense'.

When the narrator complains to a doctor about his insomnia, he is told to seek out people in 'real pain'. This is the 'Remaining Men Together: testicular cancer group' who are good examples of another kind of confused masculinity: those men who have attempted to conform to traditional roles, but who have failed.

The narrator has been emasculated by his pursuit of consumer perfection, while these men have had the symbol of their essential masculinity – referred to in Latin countries as *cojones*, literally 'bull's balls' – physically removed from them. The first speaker talks of his ambition to be a father, a goal he now will never achieve; the ultimate insult is that his wife has abandoned her emasculated husband and procreated with another man. Bob, pathetic and grotesquely breasted, is an even more pertinent example. Bob's cancer is the result of taking body-building steroids. His attempt to attain a traditional male image, the Muscle Man, has resulted in the exact opposite: Bob's physique, in reaction to the drugs he has to take, has become *feminised*, developing aptly named 'bitch tits'.

Finally, there is a third group of men in *Fight Club* – the 'solution' to the problems of confused masculinity, which eventually turns into another form of the same confusion: the neo-fascist-anarchist 'Project Mayhem' that the fight club becomes, resorting to a form of 'male fundamentalism' that is, ultimately, as empty as the other male roles it reacts against.

● Mytho-poetic essentialism

The narrator's confusion and need for a role model creates Tyler Durden – an irreverent, carefree and subversive personification of everything the narrator really wants to be. Tyler is the catalyst for a deconstruction of all the status symbols that make the narrator a 'modern man', freeing him from the distorted goals of consumer fulfilment. Firstly, the narrator's suitcase – 'my *life* is in that case' – vanishes at the airport; additionally his sexuality is slurred by the implication that his case may have contained a vibrator. Next, his apartment and all his belongings are destroyed by an explosion. All the vital symbols of his success, all the things that brought him *comfort* are suddenly erased; and this reflects his own inner emptiness back at him. As he tells Tyler in a bar immediately after:

> You buy furniture. You tell yourself, this is the last sofa I will ever need in my life. Buy the sofa, then for a couple years you're satisfied that no matter what goes wrong, at least you've got your sofa issue handled.

The narrator has 'fallen prey to the Ikea Nesting Instinct' and now that the nest has been destroyed he has to confront the numbness inside.

Tyler's intuitive response to the narrator's crisis is to suggest a far more essential emasculation: 'Could be worse. A woman could cut off your penis, and throw it out the window of a moving car…' He rejects consumerism utterly – 'the things we own end up owning us' – and invites the narrator to do the same. What Tyler's invitation resembles, on a wider cultural scale, is the call to become the kind of urban 'mytho-poetic' man discussed in the work of Robert Bly.

In his book *Iron John*, Bly talks of modern men having lost their direction because they have no role model or rite of initiation; he uses a fairytale about a prince who frees a caged Wild Man on the condition that he would become the prince's mentor and develop the 'Man' within him too. Bly said this represents the need all men have for a mentor who will teach them how to channel and express the 'Wild Man' within, a symbolic figure that is very similar to the character the narrator projects as Tyler, an *Übermensch* (superman) to awaken the 'real' man in him.

Bly also places the moment men began to lose their core identity at the beginning of the industrial age (mid- to late 19th century) when men left the family to work in factories, and the upbringing of male children fell to the mothers and peers. Throughout *Fight Club*, Tyler also attacks the feminisation of men, created not by women, but by the absence of male role models. When discussing the narrator's runaway father and the notion of marriage Tyler concludes:

> We're a generation of men raised by women … I am wondering if another woman is really the answer we need?

By removing the twin desires of money and sex, the narrator, and the other members of the fight club are able to establish themselves as men, and actualise their more primitive masculinity through physical confrontation. Crucially, though, this is not a confrontation that leads to *subjugation*, it's not about being victorious and *defeating* your opponent. The point is not to win, it is to *feel* and define yourself through that feeling: 'How do you know who you are if you've never been in a fight?'

The fighters in *Fight Club* are harking back to the pre-industrial male roles, a tribal sensibility that may not involve drum circles and sweat lodges (like many mytho-poetic men's groups) but it certainly fulfils that role. Like Bly-inspired men's groups with names like 'Male Warrior Training', the main members of Tyler's fight clubs are white middle-class achievers who feel their material successes are empty, or white working-class men who are frustrated by their lower social status. Fight Club is an *initiation* ritual – 'If this is your first time at Fight Club you have to fight' – based not around the victory of one man over another, as that would weaken the male movement by introducing opposition and competition. The focus of the fighting in *Fight Club* is *endurance* – taking the beating and defining one's identity through the pain.

Sociologists have suggested this 'trial-by-fire' initiation is still evident in our post-industrial society: the sportsman who boasts of the agonising extremes of his gym workout, the laddish pride in the severity of a hangover after a night of drinking – these acts establish masculinity through the ability to endure physical pain and discomfort. *Fight Club*'s more extreme versions are seen by Fincher as fulfilling the same function:

> … this character has a need. There's sensuality to this need and there's sensuality in this need being fulfilled. So maybe that's wrong, but it's the only way to help talk about it. The violence gives him the pain he feels. You're talking about a character who's ostensibly dead. You're talking about a guy who's been completely numb. And he finally feels something and he becomes addicted to that feeling. He has a need to feel, and that need is fulfilled by the Fight Club. (Doogan, 2000)

On the DVD commentary, Helena Bonham Carter (who plays Marla Singer in the film) talks about how the film made her think about *why* men fight, and helped her to realise that often it isn't to inflict pain as much as to prove to themselves how much pain they can stand. 'Hit me again', the narrator says over a 'post-coital' cigarette after his and Tyler's first fight; the subsequent empowerment can make 'a busboy … into a God'.

The mentality is that if you subject yourself willingly to pain, and you can cope, then the world cannot harm you (arguably a similar impulse motivates the adoption of tattoos and body piercings). A scene that exemplifies this is Tyler's goading, and the beating he receives from the gangster, Lou: he tries to intimidate Tyler, physically threaten him, but Tyler is immune; he begins to beat Tyler viciously, repeatedly, but Tyler merely laughs at the aggression, revels in the pain. Defeated by disgust at what he has wrought, and by its ineffectuality, Lou retreats.

This event is mirrored in Norton's character's self-flagellation in his boss's office, again intimidating someone who thinks they have authority with the extent of one's authority over oneself. It features again in the 'chemical burn' scene, where Tyler forces the narrator to accept and wallow in the pain, endure the agony so that he can transcend it. (Later we see all the key members of 'Project Mayhem' have similar burns, again stressing the use of pain as tribal initiation.)

One thing many critics missed in *Fight Club* is that it not only reflects, but also criticises the mytho-poetic view of masculinity. In the last 45 minutes of the film, as the fight clubs turn into anarcho-fascist terrorist cells, it becomes clear that Tyler's idealism cannot function in a real, post-industrial world (similarly, critics of Bly have said his romanticised view of pre-industrial culture ignores the harsh historical reality; the ideal is untenable in the real world). Use **Worksheet 11** to explore these ideas. The character arc of the narrator of *Fight Club* is of an adolescent experimenting with the two extremes of modern manhood – from yuppie status-slave to modern primitive – ending in eventual, responsible adulthood. *Fight Club* both explores two male relationships and follows a seminal male narrative.

To access worksheets and other online materials go to **www.bfi.org.uk/tfms** and enter User name: **menfilm@bfi.org.uk** and Password: **te2007me**.

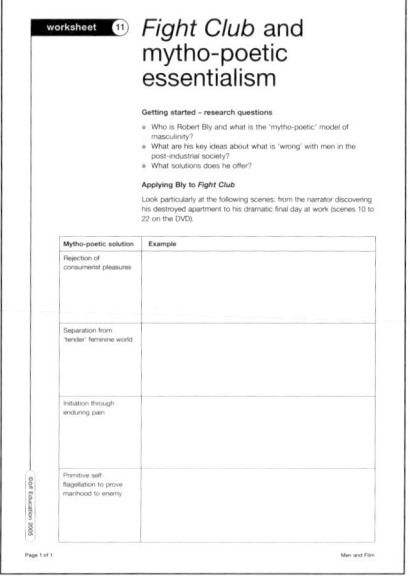

● **Male relationships**

Fight Club could also be used to examine two archetypal male relationships – acolyte and mentor/son and father – and the narratives that explore them. Reinforcing Bly's idea that part of the problem with modern men is a lack of a role model, the narrator creates Tyler from his own subconscious (Bly would say essential) needs:

● Acolyte/Mentor. Tyler is the cool kid in school: irreverent, cares nothing for status or urbane wit or etiquette. Fincher (Smith, 1999) said that he noticed that people are

> 'starting to come of age in their late twenties or thirties. In our age kids are more sophisticated at an earlier age and less emotionally capable at a later age.'

Tyler, then, is the ultimate adolescent fantasy – the 'wild man' showing the straight guy how to cut loose (familiar from the *Lethal Weapon* series and other 'buddy' movies, or from films like Richard Linklater's *School of Rock*, USA/Germany, 2003, where a 'man-boy' is able to reignite the adolescent in the over-mature adults around him).

● Son/Father. 'We are a generation of men raised by women,' states Tyler, and beyond his role as mentor, he fulfils an almost Oedipal role. His first function is to separate the narrator from the 'comfortable', feminised world: he destroys the narrator's 'nest', takes him away from the unconditional love of the support groups, and exposes him to the harsh reality of an uncaring world: 'You are not god's delicate snowflake,' etc. Like many father–son relationships though, by mentoring the 'son' in how the 'real world' is, the father reveals his own hypocrisy. This enables the 'son' to overcome and symbolically 'kill' the father and assume his own individual manhood. When the narrator shoots 'Tyler' at the climax by putting the gun in his own mouth, he is acknowledging that Tyler's weaknesses are his own, and that he now has the strength to take responsibility for them alone.

Using **Worksheet 12**, ask students to note the how the narrator and Tyler represent these male archetypes.

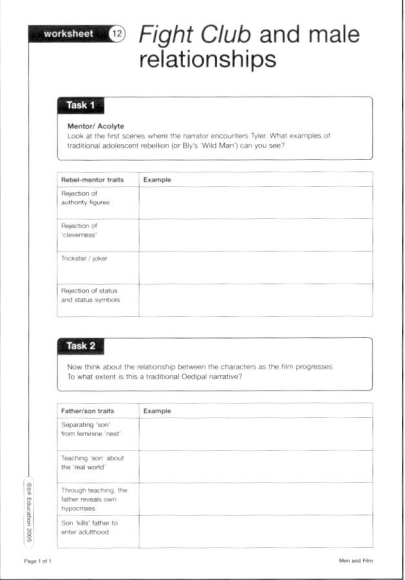

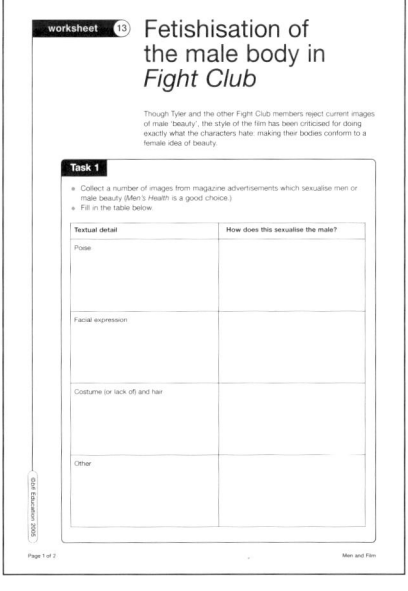

To access worksheets and other online materials go to **www.bfi.org.uk/tfms** and enter User name: **menfilm@bfi.org.uk** and Password: **te2007me**.

Ideas for further study:

● After using the worksheets to isolate how *Fight Club* tackles confused masculinity and the essentialist response to it, ask the students to collect magazine examples. Now look at the presentation of the male body in the film. Some critics have accused the aesthetic of *Fight Club* as being exactly the same as that the characters attack – is this a genuine criticism or has Fincher done this deliberately? **Worksheet 13**

● How does a male audience respond to the initial state of the narrator? Do they identify with his frustrations? Compare to *American Beauty* (Sam Mendes, USA, 1999), or *Time Out* (Laurent Cantet, France, 2001), in which a man who is fired from his job hides the fact from his friends and family because he cannot bear to disappoint the expectations they have of him. How do these films represent masculinity? How does a male audience respond to these characters? Are they able to identify with their anxieties (and weaknesses) or do they prefer to watch stronger, more aspirational roles?

Case study 2: *The Return*, brothers, fathers and sons

In this Russian thriller, Ivan, a young boy who has been brought up by his kind mother, is startled one day to find a hulking, taciturn stranger in his house. Apparently, this is his father. The 'father' takes his two 'sons' – Ivan, and his impressed older brother, Andrey – on a gruelling vacation, each uncomfortable or dangerous situation seemingly a 'lesson' to the boys in how the world really is.

This film explores male relationships and issues in a number of ways:

● It examines the formation of male identity: struggling for independence against the expectations and (unwritten) rules of mother, father, brother and peers.
● Male family relationships are explored – between fathers/father figures and sons; between brothers; between sons and mothers.
● 'Mytho-poetic' roles and narratives are enacted within a 'realist' post-Soviet environment, very different to the USA of *Fight Club*.

● Formation of male identity

There are a number of scenes that display how the events of the film are crucial in forming Ivan's identity. The first is the opening scene, where Ivan is challenged to leap from a tall, phallic tower into the sea by his brother and their friends. All the other boys have passed the test but Ivan is petrified with fear, and cannot do the leap … yet neither will he climb back down. This is the rite of passage challenge, an opportunity for Ivan to prove his 'manhood' – yet his 'failure' itself leads to a statement of physical and mental endurance: he sits, huddled at the top of the tower, half-petrified by vertigo, but also half out of obstinacy, 'digging in his heels' and refusing to fail. Finally his mother comes to 'rescue' him, and he returns to the comfort of her embrace – symbolic of the 'comfortable' feminine world he has been brought up in. Ivan repeats this strategy throughout the film: he fails and complains about most of the 'tests' set for him by his father, but these aren't signs that he has been defeated. If anything, the fact that he *dares* to complain shows his emerging identity. Ivan's expectant, then disappointed, looks at his brother indicate that this role usually belongs to Andrey, the eldest brother, but his adoration of the father silences him, forcing Ivan, though perhaps too young to voice opposition to adult plans, to take the role.

Throughout their journey, the father tries repeatedly to make Andrey take traditional male responsibilities, almost ignoring Ivan. He is requested to find a restaurant in which to eat (hunter/gatherer?) and is given the wallet to pay the bill; he is even instructed in the 'manly' way to do this – not by going up to the till, but by displaying his power over the female waitress by shouting at her to come to the table. Unfortunately, Andrey, too seems to 'fail' these tests: he takes too long finding a place to eat, the wallet is stolen by some local youths. Later, when their car gets stuck in mud, and the father gruffly orders the boys to put branches beneath the wheel, Andrey's failure results in the first explicit violence – but this is followed immediately by reward: being allowed to steer the car. In the last reel, when the boys have taken the boat out for too long, the father immediately blames Andrey (as the 'holder of his watch') despite it being obviously Ivan's fault.

The message is clear: he is the oldest, he should be the responsible man, in charge of the younger boy. His confused adoration prevents him from doing this, leaving it to Ivan to show his independence by deliberately disregarding the father's rules. When Andrey does finally accept this role, it is not to meet the father's expectations of masculinity, but rather in utter defiance of the physical violence his father is using; he takes the role of 'family protector', attacking the stranger, the threat, to protect his brother, and in doing so – it appears for a second – wins the unexpected respect of the father.

The final emergence into male adulthood is when the boys take the ultimate responsibility: for the death, and the body, of their father. As in the Oedipal narrative we discussed in *Fight Club*, the boys cannot 'become men' until the oppressive father is defeated. In *Fight Club*, this happens pseudo-symbolically (as the character isn't strictly alive in the first place); in *The Return*, though accidental, Ivan really does kill his father. And as soon as this happens, the boys are forced – through circumstance rather than brutal human action – to 'become men'. They are stranded, miles from home, on a deserted island; unless they use the skills their father had so sadistically taught them, they will not survive either. Most significant is Andrey's use of branches to lift the heavy body (learnt from using them to 'lift' the car out of the mud) down to the boat. Although they complained about rowing to the island, having done so equips them with the skill and experience to be able to 'return' themselves. Crucially, we don't see them return to the mother's love – they have matured beyond this point. Instead, the final frames are the boys' photographs of the trip, significantly focusing just on them, the father isn't pictured once; it is as if, now his lessons have been learnt, he has disappeared again, to leave the boys to their adulthood.

- Use **Worksheet 14** and the list of traditionally male values and traits (**Worksheet 2**) to look at the way Ivan and Andrey are forced to accept the 'man's role'.

To access worksheets and other online materials go to **www.bfi.org.uk/tfms** and enter User name: **menfilm@bfi.org.uk** and Password: **te2007me**.

worksheet 14 *The Return* and male identity

In your first viewing of *The Return* (Andrei Zvyagintsev, Russia, 2003), make a list of the challenges to each boy's (emerging) male identity that Ivan and Andrey undergo. Below are some ideas to start you off but try to think of your own examples.

After making a list of scenes, re-watch them, thinking about traditional masculine values and traits.

- How does Ivan fail these tests of masculinity? Write your ideas in the table.
- To what extent does he actually not fail them, but exhibits different masculine responses to the situations? Write your ideas in the table.

Challenges to masculinity	In what way does he fail?	In what way does he succeed?
Ivan – jumping from the tower into the sea		
Andrey – finding place to eat		
Andrey – rescuing car from mud		
Ivan – catching a fish		

● Male family relationships

There are a number of key scenes that explore male family relationships. Obviously, the whole film is about father and son dynamics, but the relationship between the brothers is also worth consideration.

Look at the second scene, where Ivan is taunted by his peers and brother. Although we know little about the boys' family background, the shocked look Ivan gives Andrey when Andrey mumbles 'Chicken' to agree with his friends conveys his feeling of utter betrayal. Ivan repeats this look once the father has arrived and Andrey is 'sucking up' to him: an expression of disbelief, as if the one person he could rely on has now betrayed him. In the scenes where the boys are alone in their tent at night, Ivan takes the 'older brother' role, chastising Andrey for his naïve trust and asserting his male ability to challenge the father.

The portrayal of the father, his place – long empty – in the family and the way he relates to his sons, is a very good expression of an Oedipal nightmare. We rarely see the father in any other way than through Ivan's eyes, and when we do, the audience is giving precious little extra information. To Ivan he is a figure of suspicion and fear: he gives no explanation for his 12-year absence, neither to his sons, nor to his wife. This itself plants the notion, in both Ivan's and the audience's mind, that perhaps this taciturn stranger is not the missing father at all: his cold and brutal attitude towards the sons who would love to love him, mysterious phone calls, and references to enigmatic business suggest that he may be a gangster of some sort. Look particularly at the scene where Ivan spies on him talking to the men on the pier. When he is seen carrying a long object, about the size of a small human body (a little boy?), Ivan's fears seem to be coming true; yet when this is later revealed to be an outboard motor, the threat does not fade – if anything it becomes more intense because it is unfocused.

That their father is actually an impostor is a traditional Freudian anxiety for young males; but, given Andrey's attempts to love him, we get the impression that even if he was a criminal interloper, if he gave the boys the slightest opportunity to love him then they would. Instead, he behaves like a thuggish drill sergeant, only without the articulacy of one! His communication takes the form of slaps, glares and awkward silences. Though his actions could be seen as lessons in manliness, there is no explanation of this to the boys, no phrasing of a lesson: a test is set, the boys inevitably disappoint, the father gets angry and punishes with silence or violence. (The only time he seems to 'awaken' from his cold indifference is when Ivan threatens him with the knife – the threat of violence against him, however feeble, summons an almost tender expression.)

To Ivan, then, he is a source of Oedipal fear: he forcibly removes the boys from their mother's comfortable embrace (when she 'rescues' Ivan from the tower, she says 'Of course you don't have to jump', reassuring him that such macho acts don't really win status) and subjects them to the 'cruel world' of men, forcing them through terrifying rites of passage that are also divorced of context and meaning.

That he does eventually show Ivan how to defeat his fear – Ivan threatens to leap from the tower instead of cringing back from the edge – does not, in Ivan's eyes, make him into a better father, and his death does not bring about love in retrospect.

- Using **Worksheet 15**, look at the evidence for and against this man being the boys' father. Also look at how he reflects the universal Oedipal fears.

To access worksheets and other online materials go to **www.bfi.org.uk/tfms** and enter User name: **menfilm@bfi.org.uk** and Password: **te2007me**.

worksheet 15 · *The Return* and Oedipal issues

● 'Mytho-poetic' roles in a 'primitive' environment

Just as there are similar themes to *Fight Club* in terms of Oedipal relationships, so there is also a similar implied criticism of 'mytho-poetic' male roles as advanced by Bly and Keen. They posit the pre-industrial, primitive culture as a utopian place where men and sons can bond effectively, without the modern world of work interfering; where boys have a clear role model, and are in touch with their 'natural' masculinity; where boys can go through a genuine test of physical and mental endurance to prove they can be independent. *Fight Club* shows the need for this in a postmodern, First-World (American) environment, and shows how this philosophy doesn't actually *work* in present society. Alternatively, *The Return* shows how unappealing a return to this 'primitive' world could be.

The environment – post-Soviet Russia – is bleak and harsh. Everything seems in dissolution: houses, factories and roads are crumbling; the boys who steal the wallet from Ivan and Andrey look malnourished and ill. This is a far cry from the dazzling images of capitalism that distract the men in *Fight Club*. The male characters here cannot hide behind their designer sofas – society is in decline, and they are left exposed and shivering (like Ivan with his fishing rod in the downpour). Nature is represented by the watercolour hues of the hills and lakes of northern Russia, and to the boys it is beautiful yet intimidating. No other human is evident once the father and sons leave the town – there is just nature for them to test themselves against.

In *Iron John*, Bly talks about confronting nature as a way of reaching 'core' masculinity, and as a way of bonding with other men. *The Return*, however, provides no friendship bonds for the characters to take comfort in when nature turns harsh. The rites of passage the boys have to undergo are free of context or meaning (other than in the mind of the father), so the symbolic graduation to adulthood has no resonance for the boys; they just feel like they are being bullied and abused. What *The Return* reflects is many of the criticisms levelled at Bly, that he is a romantic with a naïve view of pre-industrial society; his vision of 'primitive' societies does not take into account the social and economic challenges and seems indivisible from the Grimms' fairytales he appropriates for his purposes. The 'inventor' of the term 'mytho-poetic', Shepherd Bliss, does state clearly that:

> Rather than exploring rational, analytical, or political thinking, this approach thinks mythopoetically, ie using symbols, metaphors, and archetypal images.

Yet, he also offers Thoreau and Francis of Assisi as role models of this man who 'may throw himself onto the earth in ecstasy'. (1987)

What the *The Return* reveals is that this *is* just symbolic fantasy. When industrial society crumbles, fathers do not let out a cheer and whisk their sons onto their shoulders; they have to leave for long periods of time to seek employment elsewhere, or are forced to abandon the families they have created because they will 'slow them down'. Nature in the film *is* beautiful, but also harsh and unpredictable: the storm the boys have to row through appears from nowhere, the water eventually claims the father's body that the boys painstakingly dragged back to the mainland. *The Return* shows us the world that in the writings of Bly, Bliss and Keen should allow men to overcome the distortions, distractions and frustrations of modern life; actually it shows us a world of brutality and fear that does not offer men revitalised traditional roles, just their empty shape; and men have to find their own life within.

- Using **Worksheet 16**, look at how *The Return* tackles the ambitions of the mytho-poetic masculinity movement and exposes them as romantic ideals.

worksheet 16

The Return and 'mytho-poetic' masculinity

Think again about Robert Bly's ideas on what has caused the 'problems' in masculinity and how reverting to a more primitive, pre-industrial society, closer to nature, would cure this problem. *The Return* (Andrei Zvyagintsev, Russia, 2003) is set in an almost 'post-industrial' Russia, and the boys are put through a kind of primitive rite of passage which involves them dealing with nature, but they don't seem particularly happy about their 'empowerment'.

Fill in the table below, indicating how Andrei Zvyagintsev challenges Bly's ideas, confronting idealism with actual lives?

'Mytho-poetic' ideal	Actuality of characters' experience
Boys need father as male role model	
Boys grow up weak and confused if nurtured by mother alone	
Young men need physical and mental challenges to prove they are 'men'	
Men need to reconnect with nature in order to feel at peace	
Men need to spend time together in the wild to properly bond and form genuine relationships	

Page 1 of 1   Men and Film

To access worksheets and other online materials go to **www.bfi.org.uk/tfms** and enter User name: **menfilm@bfi.org.uk** and Password: **te2007me**.

Case study 3 – *Y tu mamá también*, machismo and maturity

Alfonso Cuarón's 2001 film *Y tu mamá también*, is interesting in that it provides us with a view of masculinity (and the pressures upon it in the postmodern world) within a different cultural context. Further than that though, the culture of machismo evident in Latin countries has traits that are recognisable in adolescent and young men in every society – and the term has been bastardised into the negative term 'macho'. *Y tu mamá también* is not only a fascinating dissection of Latino masculinity, but also a pertinent deconstruction of similar essentialist traits to those examined in *Fight Club*.

We can look at this in three ways:

- Marketing. How was the film was marketed in the US and UK to mainstream male and female audiences by appearing to celebrate adolescent machismo;
- Deconstructing machismo. Key scenes where macho traits are displayed and how they are deconstructed during the course of the characters' trip;
- Maturity. Both the role of the 'older' narrator and the link between political/social awareness and the sexual awareness provoked by Luisa.

● Marketing

In the UK and US, the film's trailers and posters virtually ignored Y tu mamá as part of the Mexican 'New Wave' and instead posited it firmly within the teen/road-movie genre. The male characters and their perspective are given prominence, with the voiceover obviously youthful instead of the mature narrator of the actual film; this level of social awareness, and Luisa's key role as more than just a male fantasy, are considerably downplayed.

The official website describes Y tu mamá as a 'teen drama', which puts it firmly in the context of other recent US movies like American Pie (Paul Weitz, USA, 1999) and Road Trip (Todd Phillips, USA, 2000). The actual film bears very little than a surface thematic similarity with these crasser movies, but the eagerness of the distributors to make these links can tell us something interesting about how a film that challenges, explores and deconstructs masculinity can lure an audience that was perhaps hoping for these traits to be reinforced.

- Show students the trailer and poster for the film (available on the DVD). How does it target a traditional male audience?
Worksheet 17

worksheet 17 **Marketing Y Tu Mamá También**

Watch the trailer for the Y Tu Mamá También (Alfonso Cuarón, Mexico, 2001).

- What are your first impressions of the film?
- Does it remind you of any other films you have seen or heard about?
- What kind of audience might be attracted to the film (try to be as specific as you can)?
- In groups of three or four, fill in the table below, sharing your ideas about target audiences and about the film's style/content.

Similar film title	Audience	Adjectives describing the style/content

Look at the lists of films and adjectives and compare them to the traditional male and female traits on **Worksheet 2**. Link the adjectives to a gender.

- Who do you think the film was marketed towards?
- How might male and female audiences interpret the trailer differently?
- How does it target both audiences?

Page 1 of 1   Men and Film

● Deconstructing machismo

Although in recent years, many Latino critics have problematised and re-appropriated the term 'machismo', the popular definition of the term is of behaviour that is 'almost overly masculine'. Writer Americo Paredes (1993) defines 'authentic' machismo as behaviour that is:

> characterized by true courage, presence of mind, generosity, stoicism, heroism, bravery

and 'false' machismo as:

> nothing but a front, false at bottom, hiding cowardice and fear covered up by exclamations, shouts, presumptuous boasts, bravado, double-talk, bombast … Supermanliness that conceals an inferiority complex. [It is an] outrageous boast, the identification of the man with the male animal, and the ambivalence toward women—varying from an abject and tearful posture to brutal disdain.

If we look at the adolescent male characters of 'teen sex comedies' from *Porky's* to *American Pie* – and in most portrayals of young men – we can see a parallel: Paredes' 'authentic'/positive machismo is the masculine ideal, circulated by tradition and the media, and what young men aspire to embody.

Meanwhile, the negative traits are the more realistic responses of men, often in response to their inability to achieve that ideal. What makes *Y tu mamá* stand out is that it not only attempts to accurately portray both sides of machismo, but it challenges and explores where these urges come from and how to cope with them.

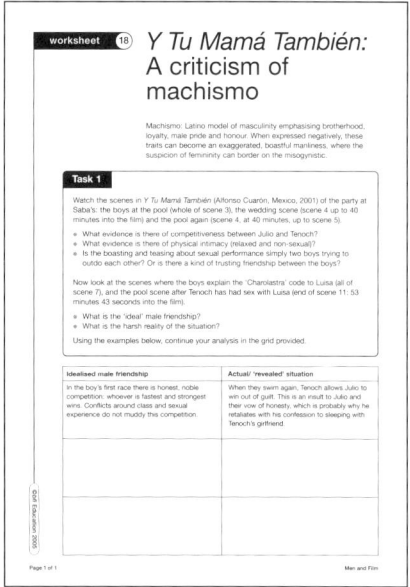

1 of 3 pages

To access worksheets and other online materials go to **www.bfi.org.uk/tfms** and enter User name: **menfilm@bfi.org.uk** and Password: **te2007me**.

Using **Worksheet 18**, watch the following scenes, then attempt to fill in the tables. There are three scenes which would make good foci for examples of both positive and negative machismo:

- The first pool scene, and the party at Saba's after. Here we see the sense of competitiveness between Tenoch and Julio: racing to orgasm, racing in the pool, and their 'horse-play' in the shower rooms display not only their ambitions to out do each other (especially from the lower-class Julio) but also their laidback physical intimacy and submerged homo eroticism. At Saba's party, they again make outrageous boasts about their capacities for drugs and sex; and again the other friend jokingly contradicts, exposing the truth of their innocence. At this stage, the machismo is adolescent, jokey and, more importantly, unthreatening: their competitiveness is not about domination and subjugation but seems to be a device for one friend to 'ground' the other, supply the reality behind the boasting. They seem to be comfortably intimate with each other's secrets though the 'mature' voiceover reveals details about the class differences between the two.

- The explanation of the 'Charolastra' code. Julio and Tenoch's reciting of their vows to Luisa is a sign of their naïve belief in the most optimistic of macho values: honour, respect, trust and a brotherhood forged by sharing experiences (getting high, sex with girlfriends) without letting these eclipse the sense of fraternity. The scene is especially useful when contrasted with:

- The second pool scene, just after Tenoch has had sex with Luisa. Here we can see the actuality behind the Charolastra's ideals. Tenoch allows Julio to win the swimming race – compromising their honesty and trust, the *intimacy* of their competition. Out of spite, Julio tells him he had sex with Ana, Tenoch's girlfriend (attempting to re-assert the sexual identity that has been injured by Tenoch's success with Luisa) – and breaking a key Charolastra code. This collapse of macho-fraternal rules is linked by the narrator to other betrayals in Tenoch's life – all examples of ideal fantasy compromised by harsh reality.

- ## Maturity

What I have omitted from the above list of examples are the challenges and changes instigated by Luisa. What raises *Y tu mamá también* above a conventional male teen drama of the 'after-that-summer-nothing–would-be-same' genre are the conclusions that are reached by the end of the film: not just personal and sexual maturity but an awareness of economic, cultural and even cosmic forces that are discussed from the reflective distance of the unnamed narrator. Though Luisa may appear – in the dramatic action of the film – to be the catalyst for the first two, her influence and the knowledge of her eventual fate also provoke the boys into the deeper level of maturity that the narrator demonstrates.

Key scenes for analysis – and those featuring less explicit sex (though the teacher should be be aware that these scenes do contain very frank discussions of sexual matters) – could be:

- Julio and Tenoch's first meeting with Luisa at the family wedding (scene 3 on the DVD). Julio's pride is affronted by Luisa's husband insulting Julio's lack of real 'life experiences'; he and Tenoch repair their egos by attempting to flirt with Luisa. To them – despite the fact that she is in her 20s – she represents the sophisticated older woman, a conquest, but virtually unattainable. To their surprise though, she is playful and friendly. The harder side of herself is demonstrated to the boys when she cuts short their youthful exuberance with a swift dismissal, exposing their naïve ambitions of seducing someone like her.

- She again punctures their machismo in scenes 8 and 9 (38–47 minutes into the film), on the first leg of their journey. They are boasting about their sexual prowess, again that youthful exuberance bubbling beyond appropriateness, and Luisa acts impressed, urging them on with a twinkle in her eye until she shocks them with her 'ever wiggle your finger…' question. Again, Luisa has fed the young men's macho egos to bursting point then exposed them as bombastic innocents.

- The final confrontation – where Luisa storms away – forces Julio and Tenoch to accept a number of revelations about their masculinity. Luisa acts as a paradigm shift, placing their childish lusts and rages in a larger context that doesn't become apparent to the boys until they discover her death. She exposes the empty nature of their sexual competitiveness, their 'macho rage' as little boys' tantrums, their 'desires' as crass and clumsy animal urges. The view of themselves as 'Latin lovers', able to seduce both young girls and experienced older women, is punctured. Most significantly she exposes the flipside of bragging sexual machismo: suppressed homosexual desire.

Luisa and the developing relationship between Julio and Tenoch force both young men to cross the barrier into manhood. Certainly, the narrative here is one of typical adolescent male fantasies: a road trip with your best buddy where you are both 'made a man' by a beautiful older woman. But by providing an older, more mature voice – possibly Julio, who wants to be a writer – the sexual and personal journey is given a depth that displays how this trip also provoked the characters' social and political awareness. Cuarón said in an interview (for Radio 4, available on the UK edition of the DVD) that these boys are almost the same person, and are locked into the single self's interior gaze. By the end of the journey, the boys have separated, become aware of their individual selves and of the bigger social and economic context of which they were ignorant at the time.

Use **Worksheet 18** to analyse scene 3, when the boys are driving past a road accident in Mexico City. There is a poignant contrast between Julio and Tenoch's juvenile 'fart' humour (familiar from the American teen comedies mentioned earlier) and the tale of the worker who was run down, a tale that illuminates a whole hidden context of the class divide in Mexico. We are left with the impression that although at the time the boys are locked in their own juvenile masculine bubble, later in life, after the events, they have the 'generosity … and presence of mind' of Paredes' constructive maschismo.

Ideas for further study:

- Compare the adolescent characters in *Y tu mamá* with those in an American film like *American Pie*. How is their machismo represented to the audience? How is teenage sexuality represented?

- Watch both films with a male and female audience. How do they respond to the men in the film, and the women? Which film's characters do the boys identify with? Did the questioning of machismo prevent them enjoying *Y tu mamá*?

- Look at representations of machismo and men in other Latin American films. Possibilities are: *City of God* (Fernando Meirelles, Brazil/France/USA, 2002), in which a boy and his friends grow to adulthood in the violent slums of Rio; *The Motorcycle Diaries* (Walter Salles, USA *et al*, 2004), the film of Che Guevara's journals, a very different model of Latino masculinity; and *Carandiru* (Hector Babenco – Brazil/Argentina, 2003), a tender but also brutal Brazilian prison movie – many of the male characters are very tough, but also gay.

Case study 4: Todd Haynes and the New Queer cinema

Todd Haynes is an interesting director to study in relation to masculinity in cinema for a number of reasons. Firstly, he is one of the most successful 'out' gay directors, winning mainstream acclaim (including four Oscar and four Golden Globe nominations for *Far from Heaven*) while firmly maintaining underground roots in experimental cinema. Secondly, his view of gay identity – and, by extension, masculinities both gay and straight – is at odds with the current pop cultural acceptance of homosexuality. Haynes adopts a confrontational and transgressive approach to representing 'gayness' that appropriates established gender roles from throughout cultural history so that they can be 'rewritten'. By using gender roles in this way, Haynes exposes the homosexual 'dark half' of established straight male types, and in so doing comments on the way masculinity is represented in our culture. His aim is to 'disrupt' the linear, accepted view of sexuality and homosexuality, by experimenting with the narrative, imagery and structure of traditional mainstream cinema. To Haynes, homosexuality is the shadow lurking underneath masculinity and how our genders are supposed to work. It's always there kind of as the culprit that is going to fuck everything up and make you feel things you don't want to feel. (Wyatt, 1998)

This view has been shared by a number of other gay directors, who have been put under the umbrella term 'New Queer cinema'

● Filmography

Superstar: The Karen Carpenter Story (USA, 1987)
Poison (USA, 1991)
Safe (USA, 1995)
Velvet Goldmine (UK/USA, 1998)
Far from Heaven (USA, 2002)

● New Queer cinema

Before we can really understand what New Queer cinema is we have to think about the 'old' version. As evidenced in Vito Russo's *The Celluloid Closet* (1981), gay men have worked in cinema since its birth, moving from the key roles they had in theatre to script, direct, compose and edit movies. Because of the taboos surrounding homosexuality and its illegal status, a clear 'gay style' was repressed, but a 'gay sensibility' was nonetheless apparent in obvious genres like the musical, but also in the 'women's films' of the 1950s and 60s (which Haynes pastiches in *Far from Heaven*), or in slipping homoerotic references past the censor by embedding them in traditionally male genres like the Western and war movies. In the social and cultural upheavals of the late 1960s and 70s, when homosexuals as well as black people and women were empowering themselves and developing a clear identity, gay directors such as Kenneth Anger and Derek Jarman adopted a radical, experimental approach, challenging the 'hetero-normative' mainstream with explicit homosexual sex and relationships.

The AIDS crisis of the 1980s, however, was the event that finally brought gay culture into collision with the mainstream. When discussing AIDS, sexuality in general had to be addressed explicitly, so the previously 'impolite' subject of alternative sexualities – and the cultures that had grown around them – was forced out of the closet and into the public discourse.

The end result of this (as discussed in Section 2) is that gay culture has drawn closer to the mainstream. Not only has 'camp' become an accepted style that is no longer necessarily gay, but homosexual characters abound in mainstream films and television, accepted and embraced members of Western society, characters who can be seen by the heterosexual audience as 'nice', non-threatening and 'just like them'.

Queer theory – analogous to Black and feminist theory in its aims to deconstruct and challenge the images of an oppressed group that the oppressors have created – is very critical of this 'mainstreaming' of gay characters. Haynes himself has stated that though he doesn't believe '*Will and Grace and Queer as Folk* don't help that kid coming out', he is suspicious that homosexuality has been 'declawed' and made an ally of the dominant cultural ideology (Mitchell, 1998). What New Queer cinema did, in the 1990s especially, was to produce films that challenged the image of the 'Rupert Everett-style gay man' who is merely 'a perfect dance partner at social functions ... where he charms straight people left and right' (Phipps, 1998).

According to queer theory, the appropriated term 'queer' itself indicates the way homosexuality has always been seen as a threat to society, something strange and dangerous. This fear reached its pinnacle during the initial Western outbreak of AIDS, but that fear mingled with the new exposure homosexual culture was receiving to 'provoke gay people to clean up their act and become inoffensive to society' so they could distance themselves from the disease – and from the associations of men's saunas and unbridled hedonism that the mainstream press referred to consistently as a factor in the spread of AIDS (Wyatt, 1998). To Haynes, this 'cleaning up' of gay life fails to express the reality of gay life and also does little to change society's view of homosexuality: in a number of interviews he has likened it to Hollywood's decision to tackle race during the 1960s, when the actor Sidney Poitier was presented as the safe, acceptable face of black culture:

> ... this gorgeous, handsome, incredibly safe depiction of black America that every liberal white person could love and embrace and put on their mantel. And again, the gay characters like Rupert Everett in *My Best Friend's Wedding* are these charming, handsome, perfect, kind of sexless characters ... (Phipps, 1998)

Haynes isn't simply reminiscing about the edgier aspects of gay life. He believes that just as Poitier's films masked 'deep conflicts of ambivalence' in America towards real black people, the positive post-AIDS depictions of gay men in the media 'do not reflect a new tolerance and acceptance in the real world' (Phipps, 1998). Haynes has said that society is still threatened by homosexuality simply because it has always been a counter-ideology, a force that 'unwrites society's rules' and subverts powerful institutions whether they be sexual, political, religious or cultural. He and other directors grouped into the New Queer cinema movement seek to restore that sense of danger and transgression that was a key experience for seminal gay artists like Jean Genet, and which still has the power to 'shiver the status quo'. Filmmakers like Gregg Araki (*The Living End*, USA, 1992 – which is subtitled *An Irresponsible Movie*) also challenge the 'heteronormative' style and structure with controversial and complex depictions of the gay experience. Haynes, after receiving the GLAAD award (for combating homophobia in the media), reiterated this viewpoint: 'If the only power we have is the power to upset the norm, then let's use it and not try to iron it out' (Gardner, 2003).

● *Superstar*

Haynes' oft-discussed, but difficult to see debut feature (there are downloadable versions on the web) is the selective biography of 1970s, icon Karen Carpenter, tracing her rise to fame, controlled by showbiz-obsessed parents, and her demise, from anorexia, at 32. The style is overly cinematic, with swooning pans and tracking shots following the characters across beautiful sets. What marks this out from the 'movie of the week' style celebrity exposé is the fact that the entire cast are Barbie dolls. The dolls are dressed in expressive costumes, and Haynes 'ages' their plastic flesh with acid as tragedy looms, depicting Karen's anorexia by paring slabs of flesh from the doll. The film was removed from distribution by the Carpenters' record label in 1989, despite Haynes saying he will only show it in schools and clinics to raise money for anorexia research.

Key points to discuss:

● Why has Haynes chosen this celebrity? What links are there between the cinematic style (pastiching Douglas Sirk's 1950s' melodramas), the Carpenters, Barbie dolls and gay culture?
● How does Haynes link the sugary public persona of the Carpenters with the dark underbelly of the 1970s?
● Haynes said he wanted 'to experiment with identification' by using dolls. Think about your personal reaction. Were you able to become emotionally involved? Does using dolls contribute to the exposition of the film's themes?
● Haynes said he was interested in the way people with diseases are defined by them. How could this link with gay life in the 1980s?

● *Poison*

Made with National Endowment for the Arts' funding that later provoked controversy, *Poison* is Haynes' most explicitly confrontational vision of homosexuality. It is divided into three, apparently disparate, stories that are intercut with each other more and more rapidly as the film continues. Confusion is avoided, however, as each section pastiches a particular film or TV genre. The story entitled 'Hero' is shot like a 'true-life mystery' TV show, about a young boy who murders his abusive father and then apparently flies out the window, never to be seen again.

In 'Horror', the style switches to camp 1950s' monster movie: a scientist, Dr Graves, isolates a liquid form of the human sex drive which he accidentally ingests; he mutates into a pus-oozing sex-crazed monster, rampaging through the bars and alleyways of a city, infecting others with the disease, until a bloodthirsty mob hunts him down.

'Homo' is a homage to Jean Genet's brutal–erotic prison stories, showing the tender–cruel relationship between two prisoners; flashbacks to the borstal where they were earlier incarcerated are shot through a deep red filter, giving them a sinister kind of rosy colour, while the present-day prison scenes are metallic blue. The film climaxes with the prisoner, Broom, reminiscing fondly about a day at the borstal where he lay on the ground and bullies spat on his face and in his mouth – curiously, though, this is portrayed in dreamy slow motion, the faces of the boys angelic against a blue sky, the gobbets of spit sending the adolescent Broom into ecstasy.

Key points to discuss:

- The act of naming in the film is very important. Contradictory accounts from neighbours and schoolmates label the boy in the first story both 'a liar' and 'a gift from God'; the once respectable scientist is dubbed the 'Leper Sex Murderer' in the press; and Broom is forced to accept the label 'homosexual' when he first arrives in the prison. What might Haynes be trying to say about the way society reacts to those who break its rules?
- To what extent could this be said to be a film about AIDS?
- Haynes described *Poison* as a 'hymn to transgression'. Why is transgressing so important to him as a gay filmmaker?
- One of the stories is inspired by the work of Jean Genet. Who was this writer? What were his views of sexuality? How do his themes link to the other two stories?
- The scenes of Dr Graves' ridiculously grotesque oozing are mirrored by Broom's ecstatic memory of being showered with phlegm. The tone shifts abruptly from 'horror' to 'homo'erotic. What is Haynes trying to say about gay desire and the way straight society perceives it?
- Haynes is again appropriating the styles of three different film/TV genres. Why has he chosen these particular genres?

● *Safe*

Haynes' third film is perhaps the least obviously 'gay', though it more thoroughly explores themes of disease, the need for society to label and the experience of being placed – by a condition – outside 'normal' society. *Safe* is the story of Carol White, an upper middle-class suburbanite whose bland, wealthy, empty life seems similar to that of a 'Stepford Wife': she lunches, she goes to aerobics, she picks up dry cleaning, she cradles her husband tenderly but passionlessly as he literally humps her. And then she gets sick. Inexplicably, the chemicals used in dry cleaning, in beauty products, the exhaust fumes on the highway begin to afflict Carol, jerking her out of her doll-like existence. After frustrating encounters with shrugging doctors, one expert tells Carol she has an 'allergy to the 20th century', to the 6,000 plus chemicals that surround and penetrate our modern existence. The second half of the film takes Carol to a New Age therapy retreat, where the aim is to be 'clear': free from anything that pollutes. Here, patients are persistently urged by the self-help guru, Dunning, to accept responsibility for their conditions, not to blame society. As an audience, we are caught between loathing for this psycho-babble and hope for Carol as, by taking responsibility for her illness, she also takes control of her existence, maybe for the first time.

Key points to discuss:

- There are hardly any close-ups of the characters at all, and lots of extreme, wide-angled shots. Why? How does Haynes engage our empathy with Carol?
- The theme of labelling is again apparent in the first half of the film, as Carol's husband, friends and doctors struggle to name her condition. Later, Carol says she can't join in with a therapy session because she 'doesn't quite know the words yet'. How important is language for understanding? Are there – and should there be – experiences beyond language?
- Though we regard Dunning's words with cynicism, Haynes doesn't give us any counterpoint to disprove what he is saying, which prevents this character from becoming satirical. Why has he done this?

● *Velvet Goldmine*

Possibly as far as possible from *Safe*'s austere, almost clinical tone, where the empty, lonely spaces of modern buildings nearly overwhelm the emotional intensity, *Velvet Goldmine* is as loud, confrontational and superficial as the glam rock era it portrays. The plot, concerning a journalist investigating the faked death publicity stunt of a David Bowie-esque rock star, is an excuse to bring a 21st-century visual style to a subculture that would have wallowed in the grandiose excesses of contemporary pop videos. As various wasted ex-rock associates flashback the history of Brian Slade's rise to bisexual, androgynous celebrity, the story not only gets lost, but does so via references to gay aliens, Oscar Wilde and sexual liberation (or at least its affectations). Again, Haynes appropriates a cultural style that confronts masculinity and sexuality, but in *Velvet*, unlike his previous films, the transgressive 'perversion' of homosexuality is beautified and glamorised. It retains its subversive quality but revels in kitsch, comically showing straight society's horrified reaction.

Key points to discuss:

- How is fashion and performance used to attack the mainstream throughout the film?
- Haynes has said that glam rock involves playing roles and drawing attention to the fact that we all play roles every day. Look at the narrator (or Brian Slade). What are the different roles he plays throughout the film? What prompts him to adopt these roles? What is Haynes trying to say about the 'performative' nature of gender?
- The film itself, from the unusual opening scene on, plays at being many different things, more so even than *Poison*. List the different genres it seems to travel through (eg fairytale, rock star exposé, detective story, coming-of-age confessional, pop video) Now look at the following quote from Haynes:

> … to me it's liberating to not think of identity as some organic property that we have to find and stick to, but actually something that is constructed, or that's imposed, that we can then counter by taking a different route and re-dressing it, and then re-dressing it again, and then re-dressing it again. It's like having every possibility at your fingertips, as opposed to some natural sense of who we'll be imprisoned by for the rest of our lives. Maybe dad dresses up as dad every day. (Mitchell, 1998)

How has Haynes gone beyond merely making a film that features characters who behave in this way? How does this link with some of the ideas behind New Queer cinema?

● *Far from Heaven*

Haynes' most accessible film and his most acclaimed, even winning Oscar nominations, *Far from Heaven* is a deceptively straightforward homage to the Douglas Sirk melodramas he more viciously pastiched in *Superstar*. The style is lyrical bordering on kitsch: Julianne Moore's character, Cathy, wears a russet and rose-red ensemble that matches the two shades of autumnal leaves behind her; her husband's green-grey suit is mirrored in the green walls of his office and the steely desk that dominates it. It is easy – especially as nothing particularly dramatic seems to occur in the opening scenes – to get lost in the surface detail, almost like a heritage film in the visual pleasures of lavish texture, colour and shadow it offers. This is, however, part of the point.

The viewer is put in the position of Cathy: dazzled by her superficial surroundings. Cathy is the perfect wife, with the perfect family (children who beg to stay up past 7pm and when denied respond with 'Ah, gee…') and the perfect husband. Named after the corporation at which Frank is an executive, and indicative of the wealth such businesses brought to the 1950s, US suburbs, they are crowned 'Mr and Mrs Magnitech' by a local society magazine. When she discovers Frank's late office hours are actually spent seeking liaisons with gay men – and when Cathy herself crosses her society's boundaries by beginning a tentative relationship with her black gardener – both she and the audience are shocked by how paper-thin the artifice has been. Our senses have been fooled by the richness of the surface. Cathy's world, as carefully constructed as her home and wardrobe, begins to crumble, and – as with Haynes' other films – the roles that we play for ourselves and each other are taken apart in the process. Haynes cleverly illustrates the hypocrisies and prejudices towards homosexuality by linking them to the equally transgressive issue of mixed-race relationships.

Haynes ensures that we empathise with this 'normal' woman who is suddenly cast by her community as a deviant; in doing so, he doesn't challenge us head-on with 'deviancy' as in his earlier films. Instead, we – through our empathy with Cathy – are forced to see how deviancy is not a 'condition'. Rather, he shows how a society creates the *role* of the 'deviant', around emotions and actions which seem perfectly acceptable, and worse still, emotionally fulfilling for the protagonists. Instead of confronting a mainstream audience with transgression, he invokes their empathy with the transgressors.

Key points to discuss:

- Find examples of the characters inhabiting roles. How do they play them? What evidence is there in the first half of the film that they are uncomfortable within them?
- Note the camera movement, especially the 'up, up and away' tracking shots. How does this visual motif link to the themes of being caged and of escape (and flight?) of his earlier films?
- Examine the portrayal of homosexuality. How do the camera angles and *mise en scène* in the scenes in the gay bar create a feeling of unease? How does this link later to Frank's 'treatment' with his doctor? Is this quite threatening representation reminiscent of the portrayals in *Poison*? How does this help us to empathise with Cathy?

● Ideas for further study

- Compare Haynes' work with that of another gay director who works more closely with the mainstream. A good choice would be Gus Van Sant. Look at his more experimental films (*My Own Private Idaho*, USA, 1991) and his more 'normal' (*Good Will Hunting*, USA, 1997). To what extent is Van Sant a 'gay' filmmaker? Are there still 'gay' elements in his more mainstream films? An interesting comparison to Haynes' appropriation of film styles from the 50s and 60s would be Van Sant's shot-by-shot remake of *Psycho* (USA, 1998).
- Compare *Poison* with the autobiographical 'psychedelic' documentary *Tarnation* (Jonathan Caouette, USA, 2004). In what way do they both experiment with form and style to create a 'Queer' cinema?

Case study 5: Paul Verhoeven

Verhoeven would make an ideal counterpoint to an auteur study of Todd Haynes for a number of reasons. Firstly, Verhoeven is a heterosexual director who clearly markets to men. Akin to Haynes, however, he trades in already established male roles (the frazzled detective, the femme fatale, the tough space commando) but deconstructs these roles as his narratives progress. Secondly, Verhoeven creates an interesting relationship with his (mostly male) audience, luring them into the cinema by targeting their traditional masculine desires, giving them exactly what they wanted … but to a degree that makes them very uncomfortable, so making them reflect on the desires the initial marketing had exploited.

Another reason that Verhoeven is an interesting filmmaker is his status as one of the most successful European directors in America. Critics have often placed him in a tradition of European directors who move to America not to 'sell out' but rather to bring an 'outsider's' perspective to American culture and society. Fritz Lang satirised the American dream in *Sunrise* (USA, 1927), Douglas Sirk manipulated the genre of melodrama to comment on the repressed tensions in 1950s' American society, while Milos Forman (*The People vs Larry Flynt*, USA, 1996; *Man on the Moon*, USA, 1999) attacked American moral hypocrisies and the relationship of the individual with society. Verhoeven parodies the excesses of sex and violence in the media that the American sexual identity seems to depend upon, working within traditionally 'male genres' in order to subvert them. As Xavier Mendick (2002) comments:

> The typical Verhoeven male finds himself in situations in which his sense of identity, sexuality and past, are profoundly undercut by either duplicitous individuals or corrupt social structures.

Not only is masculinity being deconstructed here, but also men's relationship with traditional gender roles, and with (especially American) society as a whole. As Verhoeven's films are, superficially, more accessible than Haynes', the teacher with a lower ability or less adventurous students may find it easier to use texts like *Starship Troopers* or *Total Recall*. This doesn't mean that they cannot be used to approach difficult theory (on the contrary, a film like *Hollow Man* could almost be co-scripted by Mulvey, it explores male spectatorship so obviously) and, as the *Basic Instinct* example shows, Verhoeven's films can be used to introduce difficult ideas, while their moral ambiguity can provoke discussion of theoretical positions. Although Verhoeven's earlier Dutch films are interesting in their own right and do contain evidence of his early themes – violent Christian imagery in *The Fourth Man*, the sexually empowered heroine of *Flesh and Blood* – I will be concentrating on his American films, their portrayal of gender, and their relationship with both a hetero- and homosexual male audience.

● **Filmography**

Turkish Delight (Netherlands, 1973)
Keetje Tippel (Netherlands, 1975)
Soldier of Orange (Belgium/Netherlands, 1977)
Spetters (Netherlands, 1980)
The Fourth Man (Netherlands, 1983)
Flesh and Blood (Spain/USA/Netherlands, 1985)
RoboCop (USA, 1987)
Total Recall (USA, 1990)
Basic Instinct (USA, 1992)
Showgirls (France/USA, 1995)
Starship Troopers (USA, 1997)
Hollow Man (USA, 2000)

● **Introducing Verhoeven: Interrogation scene in *Basic Instinct***

This scene is not only an accessible introduction to issues surrounding the male gaze and representations of sexual dynamics, it can be used as an analogy for the relationship between Verhoeven's films and their male audience.

Nick Curran (Michael Douglas), a San Francisco detective with a few skeletons in his closet, has just brought in Catherine Trammel (Sharon Stone), a best-selling novelist, for questioning. She is the suspect in a murder case: her ex-lover has been found, tied to a bed, stabbed repeatedly with an ice-pick – a scene described by Trammel in her last novel.

Two key elements have already been established. Voyeuristic pleasure has been aroused in a previous scene where Curran waits for Trammel to change, peeking through a crack in her bedroom door (shot from his point of view) and catching Trammel naked, with her back to us, slipping into a dress; the 'male gaze' is teased by a glimpse, but then denied full view. At the same time the opening murder with the phallic ice-pick, and Trammel's empowered flirtation with Curran in the car on the way to the police station, has already marked this woman as a potential threat to the male spectator's ego.

The smug smiles and roving eyes of the all-male interrogators when Trammel first enters reflect the audience's desire for her. And, as if to satisfy this, Trammel is seated in a set design that recalls a pole-dance show more than a police interview room. She is on centrestage, elevated and brightly spotlit, the men in the room (like the men in the cinema audience) are in shadows; she is exposed to their gaze, they are hidden in their spectatorship.

What Trammel, and Verhoeven, do with the male spectatorship next undermines all our expectations. Firstly, as the detectives inquire about her sexual habits, Trammel not only meets their (and the camera's) eye, she addresses them/us directly too: 'Exactly what did you have in mind?' The question is half-tease, half-challenge; when the now-awkward interrogator is more specific, Trammel is happy to go into far more detail than they wish. She recognises the men's desire, and turns it back on them. Her refusal to put out her cigarette also marks her out as a wielder of phallic power, not a victim of it.

Secondly, as Trammel continues to flirt-challenge – referring to Curran's personal life, 'talking dirty' in her descriptions of her relationships – she crosses and uncrosses her legs, flashing her pubes at both the men in the room, and in the cinema audience. The discomfort this causes her interrogators is obvious: they shuffle, their eyes bulge, sweat darkens their shirts, even Curran slumps back almost defeated. From this point onwards, the scene's erotic potential is spent: the way Trammel still draws attention to her long legs but her pose is traditionally 'confident masculine': ankle on knee, hands dropped down by her sides, tapping the chair.

How does this reflect Verhoeven's relationship with his male audience? Here as with films like *Showgirls* and *Hollow Man*, the desire for voyeuristic spectatorship is deliberately targeted in the film's marketing; the 'beaver shot' of *Basic Instinct* became a tabloid *cause célèbre* in the weeks prior to the film's release, the grainy photos that accompanied were teasingly unclear. I Q Hunter, in a cult-media.com article, said that:

> The subtext of *Basic Instinct*'s notorious leg-crossing scene is, 'What you really want is to see Sharon's cunt – well, here it is.'

Although that may have been the subtext of the entire film's marketing campaign, the interesting thing here is that the exposure is not satisfying, neither to the men in the scene, nor – if the male audience have, as suggested by Mulvey, been identifying with their on-screen avatar's desire – to the male spectators in the cinema.

This is a device Verhoeven uses again and again – not just in regard to sex, but also in regard to the audience's desire to witness explicit violence. He packs his films with excesses, often mingling both sex and violence, and it is on the promise of such content that the films are marketed; yet by giving the spectator *more* than they desire to see, he deliberately provokes discomfort. Voyeuristic desire is encouraged, but then frustrated, not by challenging male desire with the threat of castration (as Mulvey sees the male reaction to empowered, active women characters), but by meeting those desires in such an excessive, parodic way as to almost 'embarrass' the spectator for feeling such desires in the first place. In this way, Verhoeven can exploit male desire and *criticise* it, while still making commercially successful films in established Hollywood genres.

Recap on Mulvey's theories, and watch this scene again. Use **Worksheet 19** to comment on how this scene fulfils Mulvey's ideas about the presentation of women for the 'male gaze'. Then comment on how it subverts these ideas.

● *RoboCop*

Verhoeven's first Hollywood film epitomises and introduces his love/hate
relationship with American culture. His wife apparently rescued the script from
their wastebin and urged him to take another look, and to think about how he
could use it to comment on the 'idiotic culture' he had been confronted with
as a new arrival in the country. *RoboCop* is set in a future (though now our
past) 1999 Detroit where the collapse of public funding and a surge in crime
leads to the police force being privatised, and run by OCP, a corporate
contractor. Murphy, a cop newly transferred to Detroit, is barely introduced
before he is viciously gunned down by a criminal gang. Although his limbs are
completely destroyed he clings to life. As part of OCP's plan to clean up old
Detroit and clear the way for corporate development, Murphy's remains are
used as the basis for 'the future of law enforcement'. Part organic, part
machine, RoboCop emerges as a virtually indestructible titanium sheriff: he
twirls his pistol like a gun-slinger, and utters John Wayne Western clichés like
'Dead or alive you are coming with me'. He seems to be a fantasy of
exaggerated masculinity; an invulnerable physique, superhuman strength, and
nearly emotionless, yet, unlike Schwarzenegger's Terminator, he has a
profound moral sense. In psychoanalytic terms, he should reinforce the ego of
the traditional male spectator, embodying all the key male status traits:
strength, honour, loyalty, endurance.

The subplot of *RoboCop*, however, contradicts this. Like the soldier and the
sheriff before him, RoboCop is not an independent force; he is controlled by

an institution whose concerns may not always be as moral as his own. Further than this, though, RoboCop is a *product*. OCP created him as a prototype, a test model, like the ED-209 that malfunctions so spectacularly at the film's start. Even his strict morality is compromised by the 'directives' that unconsciously corrupt his ability to 'be a good cop'. Struggling against this is the remaining psyche of Murphy, an old-fashioned hero, who became a victim of his body's inability to match the expectations of his role – a more cynical, more modern man may not have put himself in the situation that led to Murphy's demise. Reborn as RoboCop, physical vulnerability no longer restrains him but emotional vulnerability does. RoboCop has memory flashes as he sleeps – the audience sees them from his perspective – of who 'Murphy' was; not the invulnerable urban sheriff but a warm husband, intimate lover and tender father.

Throughout the film, as RoboCop's titanium invincibility is tested by various assaults by his enemies, and as his armour gradually falls apart, so his 'real' self emerges. By the end of the film, he has balanced the conflicting male impulses of violence, strength, loyalty with emotion, vulnerability, the need for family and intimacy. Angela Ndalianis (2001) says that RoboCop embodies a new 'cyborg' masculinity – a male figure that represents many positive traditional traits and who, after a struggle, is now fully in touch with his (humanising) emotions. He is able to deal with a threatening capitalist (the hoods who killed Murphy work for OCP) and technological world because he also accepts that he is a *product* of that world.

Key scenes to discuss:

- Look at the scene where Murphy is tortured. Verhoeven said this was meant to resemble a crucifixion, ritualised violence ending one life and starting another. To what extent could this be seen as a similar portrayal of violence to that in *Fight Club*, as a 'rite of passage' needed for Murphy to become a 'man'? What does the 'man' he becomes tell us about expectations of men in the postmodern world?
- Now look at the scenes where Murphy's body is being salvaged, where the OCP executives order the scientists to 'lose the good arm', replacing Murphy's uninjured organic body for a more 'efficient' machine engineered by the corporation. Think about the changes to masculine values and roles that have taken place in industrial and post-industrial society. What does this scene, and others, suggest about the nature of the male body and traditional masculine values in the 21st century? How does a male audience respond to these scenes?
- Examine the scenes after RoboCop's betrayal when he is recovering with Lewis. Why is it significant that Lewis, Murphy's cop partner, is a woman, especially during the latter part of the film when RoboCop is in recovery? Would this scene have worked if Lewis had been male? How 'masculinised'

is this character throughout? Considering that she is never sexualised or seen as a romantic possibility, how does a male audience respond to her?

- Compare RoboCop's first night on the job with Sarah Connor's speech in *Terminator 2: Judgement Day* (James Cameron, USA, 1991) about how the Terminator could be the 'ultimate father' to John. How do male audiences respond to the expectations of strong male roles modelled in these films?

● *Total Recall*

The success of *RoboCop* led to Verhoeven again tackling issues like capitalism and masculine identity in a sci-fi setting, with the additional star power of Arnold Schwarzenegger – an actor who himself has connotations of exaggerated (and problematic) masculinity. Again, the male spectator is attracted to a marketing campaign that featured the dependable action hero, a controversial level of violence and ground-breaking special effects. In an almost macho announcement, *Total Recall* also boasted of being the most expensive motion picture ever made. As with *RoboCop*, the expectations of the audience are both met and exceeded, while questions of male desire (and that includes aspiration) and identity are explored ... in between the shoot-outs.

Total Recall begins with Schwarzenegger as Quaid, a dissatisfied construction worker on a future Earth, where space travel to the colonies of Mars is a part of everyday life. Frustrated with his dull life (this banality somehow also includes Sharon Stone as his wife) he goes to ReKall Inc., a new breed of leisure company which can implant memories of a perfect, and far more exciting, holiday instead of your physical body going on a more pedestrian 'real' vacation. The advert Quaid sees promises 'the bottom of the sea, ... the mountains of Mars' but when he gets to ReKall he realises they can actually sell him his dreams: he can spend his holiday anywhere, doing anything, and more importantly as *anybody*. The consumer can design a narrative and then 'buy' the memory of it – very much like the postmodern view of identity. Quaid picks the memory of a typical male fantasy figure: a James Bond-style spy, chased by evil assassins but with a tough, beautiful woman by his side. When the technicians try to implant the memory, however, something goes wrong – apparently there already is an implant, replacing Quaid's true self ... who really *is* a secret agent. From this point on, the audience isn't entirely sure whether they are witnessing an implanted narrative – it certainly follows the conventions of 'male' genres like the Western, spy, action and sci-fi movie – nothing more than Quaid's fantasy, or whether this is actual 'reality'. At one point, the ReKall scientist appears out of the blue to warn Quaid that he is undergoing a 'schizoid embolism' that has trapped him in his fantasy; just before Quaid kisses his love interest over a beautiful red Martian dawn, he comments on the unreality of the scene: 'What if this is just a dream?'

71

As in *RoboCop*, Verhoeven has set up a dissonance between idealised male body and identity, and again made free-market capitalism its source. Schwarzenegger's almost superhuman strength had, by this point, been established in a slew of action movies, reinforcing the machinic invulnerability of his Terminator role. The success of this role with male audiences had, by *Total Recall*, made him very wealthy and established him as one of Hollywood's stars. And certainly, the role of the ruthless *Übermensch* is very much played in *Total Recall*. But, like the violence in *RoboCop* and the sex in *Showgirls*, the role is exaggerated into parody: after the (failed?) first implant, Quaid stops being 'himself' and becomes like a character in a video game in the segue scenes between levels: it is 'you' moving, but it's on autopilot, following an unconscious pattern that has been injected (like RoboCop's directives). He is a male fantasy of strength, skill, bravery and (oddly for the actor) supposed sexual allure; but the 'real' identity, 'Everyman' Quaid, is suppressed within. Like RoboCop, he has physical invulnerability but psychologically and emotionally he is in turmoil.

Key points to discuss:

- Look at the narrative's use of Western genre conventions once Quaid gets to Mars: the train into 'Venusville', which is itself a frontier town full of saloons, brothels and bar brawls; Cohaagen as the 'evil cow rancher' holding the community in his grip until Quaid, the 'stranger' appears. What other 'male' genres does the film borrow imagery and conventions from? What does this tell you about the film's marketability? How might Verhoeven be using these to subvert the typical 'male' film?
- How does a male audience feel about Quaid's position at the following points in the narrative: at the start of the movie (is being a builder really so bad if you are married to Sharon Stone?); after his first encounter with the enemy agents; when he is revealed as a potential saviour of the Martians; the 'schizoid embolism' scene; and the romantic finale?
- At what points does the audience identify with him? When are they confident about his success, and when do they worry for him? How do they respond to the disorientation invoked by being placed *within* Quaid's unstable perspective? Would they prefer a more stable generic narrative?
- How does Verhoeven's vision of masculine identity link to postmodernism and its impact on gender roles?

● *Basic Instinct*

Though there is a fuller discussion of *Basic Instinct* above, there are a number of other issues regarding men, gender and sexuality that could be explored. (Note that though the film was controversial at the time of release, the 'explicit' sex and nudity is now fairly commonplace on UK television, though, as with many of the films in this guide, discretion is advised with more sensitive students).

Other key scenes that would form a good basis for discussion are the 'date rape' scene where Curran and his ex-girlfriend have sex, those in the gay club and those featuring Roxy, Trammel's girlfriend. Before viewing the scenes, advise students to read the Stirling Media Group's research into 'Men Viewing Violence'. This is a revealing and extremely readable study, with very little critical jargon (available at www-fms.stir.ac.uk/research/mvv/index.html).

Key points to discuss:

- The 'Men Viewing Violence' study found that heterosexual men and gay men viewed Catherine Trammel differently. Both recognised that the sex and nudity was framed within the 'male gaze', but the straight men enjoyed this while the gay men distanced themselves from this element and took pleasure in seeing a strong and sexually empowered woman subvert gender roles. What does this tell you about the way gay and straight audiences relate to both gendered characters and separately, to the gendered perspective?
- How does the interrogation scene seem to conform to Mulvey's ideas while actually subverting them?
- Watch the ambiguous 'rape' scene again. To what extent is this portrayed as an actual rape? To what extent is it portrayed as 'rough sex' to titillate the male viewer?
- Look at the 'Men Viewing Violence' male subjects' response to this scene. The ambiguity seems to provoke reflection on what constitutes rape and on how the male subjects were emotionally manipulated by the film, identifying with Curran's disempowerment after Trammel's interview, and the need to reassert his male sexual dominance, but also questioning it. What does this tell us about the way Verhoeven uses controversial sexual and violent content?
- Curran is actually a very conservative character, especially when it comes to sexuality. He seems shocked that a woman can 'fuck' for pleasure not love, he consistently denigrates gay men and he is extremely suspicious of Catherine's bisexuality. The film also caused demonstrations from ACT UP on its release, which accused it of being homophobic. How do straight and gay male audiences respond to the portrayals of homosexuality in the film? How do they respond to 'deviancy' that caters more to traditional male fantasies (mild bondage, femme fatales and 'lipstick' lesbians)?

● *Showgirls*

While the satirical content of *Starship Troopers* is no longer in doubt, there are fewer critics who can appreciate the parody in *Showgirls*, perhaps because it is still – even after the crass marketing of the equally crass *Basic Instinct* – the most cynically targeted of his films. Joe Eszterhas wrote what seemed like a movie phenomenon: a film that would take soft porn to the mainstream, and would welcome instead of cringe from the dread NC-17 rating, bringing the NC-17-rated movie to the multiplex. Unfortunately, this strategy backfired – the reason why home video killed the porn theatre is because ultimately the relationship between spectator and explicit pornography is a private one, usually shamefully denied rather than proudly exhibited in the social space of the cinema. That was not the end of *Showgirls*, however. The film enjoyed a big success in the New York gay and drag scene as a successor to *The Rocky Horror Show* (Jim Sharman, USA, 1975): a new print was issued (similar to 'Sing-a-long-a *Sound of Music*') with appalling dialogue subtitled so that the audience could 'say-a-long' the script and musical numbers inspired by the movie bookended performances.

Showgirls is the tale of Nomi Mallone, a mixture of contradictory naivety and street sass who claws her way up the stripping ladder, from lapdancing at dive bars to being the biggest top-billed topless starlet in Vegas. Verhoeven takes the showbiz rags-to-riches story of *All About Eve* (Joseph L. Mankiewicz, USA, 1950) and the musical numbers of *42nd Street* (Lloyd Bacon, USA, 1933) and turns everything up to a crazed volume and pace, interspersing deliberately soulless and mechanical sex scenes between virtually every event. This may be his most cynically marketed film, but it is one of his most cynical in attitude, too. Women's bodies are the same as currency – the price of employment at the Cheetah Bar is to give the manager a blowjob; the price of an audition is to take part in a humiliating display of breasts. Nomi's breaking point comes when her best friend is virtually 'given' to one of the casino's big stars to gang rape. Yet, far from allowing themselves to be exploited, the women in *Showgirls* use their bodies as currency to get what they desire – material wealth, fame and sexual worship. Nomi gyrates passionlessly at every man (or woman) who could possibly further her 'career'. These are not Mulvey's passive victims of the male gaze; they thrust their objectified bodies into the faces of the male audience, making them feel as exploited by paying to see this display as the male characters in the film.

Key points to discuss:

- How do male spectators feel towards Nomi at the film's start, where we see her both tough and vulnerable. What traditionally masculine and feminine traits does she exhibit throughout the film? Can men in the audience identify with her? Are there any men in the film that the male viewer is encouraged to identify with? How do gay men respond (especially considering the later reputation of the film as a 'camp classic')?
- How do male audiences respond to the lapdance and sex scenes? Do they have the same reaction to the sex scenes in *Basic Instinct*? How do the scenes make men feel about the status of the women in the film?

- Xavier Mendick (2002) comments that Verhoeven's female characters are strong women

  'whose bonds with other females function to exclude the depicted male hero from the domains of knowledge and sexual power'.

  How is this exhibited in *Showgirls*, compared to *Basic Instinct* or the less sexual *Starship Troopers*?

● *Starship Troopers*

Once the outcry caused by the *Washington Post*'s ridiculous misinterpretation – 'This is a fascist film' – had died down, *Starship Troopers* became one of Verhoeven's most critically acclaimed and popular films. Perhaps this is because, finally, many 'got the joke': that a film that appeals to violent sensibilities can also satirise those same sensibilities. As with *Total Recall*, *Starship Troopers* merges conventions from the Western (the attack on the fort is a sci-fi replay of *Drums along the Mohawk*, John Ford, USA, 1939), the World War II movie (the training, the first big battle, the graduation through the ranks) and big-budget sci-fi – all typically male genres, where aggression and conflict are used to resolve issues. 'It's simple folks – we're in it for the species,' states one army officer, and that, deceptively, is the attraction: a simple humans versus aliens fight. The teaser trailer that Verhoeven used to persuade the studio to make the film was also used in the initial marketing: a futuristic soldier walks along a sandbank, glancing around him – suddenly a huge, mean and *fast* bug scampers onto screen, claws and legs a near-blur, dismembering the soldier in seconds before turning and launching itself at the camera. The studio said 'Yes', and so did audiences – they could smell blood, and uncomplicated blood at that.

But what Verhoeven does in *Starship Troopers* is different to his other violent sci-fi spectaculars. He doesn't just confront us with more violence than we can bear. Because the film is so parodic, the extremity of violence actually becomes humorous in its ferocity. Verhoeven encourages us to enjoy the dismemberments and eviscerations but immediately after the slam-bang opening, he takes us back in time to show us the social context. What would a society look like that could authorise, encourage and celebrate such violence, while not descending into savagery? We are introduced to a scary future by a teacher, Mr Rasczak:

  We've talked about the failure of democracy. How the social scientists brought our world to the brink of chaos. We talked about the veterans, how they took control and imposed the stability that has lasted for generations since.

This is a world where the bombing of Hiroshima is celebrated, where signing up to the military is the only way to be a 'citizen' (and only citizens can have children) and where criminals are executed 'live' nightly on every channel. This is certainly a fascist world Verhoeven is portraying and not just in its politics; it seems the fat, the ugly and the non-white have been eradicated along with the 'failed' democracy. The main characters are supposed to Argentinian, yet they have the cosmetic beauty of Californian soap actors (cleverly, Verhoeven casts *actual* day- and evening-soap actors) and speak American English; there is no evidence of Latino features beyond their names (Rico, Carmen). It is a portrait of the world after globalisation has run its course, where ethnicity and 'difference' has disappeared … although strangely so has sexual difference: the male and female soldiers all bunk and shower together, and many of the Sky Marshals and pilots are women.

Verhoeven again lures an audience with the promise of uncomplicated action and violence but then confronts them with the surface aesthetic of the American Dream – chiselled jaws and bulging biceps for the men, huge eyes and bright white smiles for the women – but with the narrative of Nazi propaganda: the celebration of brute strength over weakness is American machismo with an Aryan heart. But this is the culture of violence, the society of violence that the audience has paid to see, violence that is not comfortably decontextualised, but linked historically and socially to the West's past. Bearing in mind the 'Americanised' Earth *Starship Troopers* presents, and the very real recent wars in Afghanistan, Iraq (and 'on Terror'), it also uncomfortably reflects our present.

Key points to discuss:

- Watch the trailer for *Starship Troopers*. What does a male audience find attractive?
- What are a male audience's views on the society portrayed? Show the scenes in the high school and at the ball, but with the volume turned down: how do they respond to the aesthetics? Now restore the volume: How do they react to the politics of this future?
- Discuss the representation of men and women. How do male and female audiences respond to the strong women? Can both sexes identify with Carmen or Dizzy? Do they feel the women have been sexualised (especially in the shower scene)?
- The male body is once again made incredibly strong, but it is also the property of an authoritarian institution, this time the army. Look at the scene after the first attack on Klandathu, where Rico is declared dead and then repaired, ready for battle again. How does this compare to the other near indestructible but corporate-owned heroes of *Total Recall* and *RoboCop*?
- Look at a summary of Klaus Theweleit's *Male Fantasies Volume 2: Psychoanalyzing the White Terror* at http://www.georgiasouthern.edu/~lamy/teaching/gender/SVC/Thiewalt.htm. Theweleit wanted to understand, from a Freudian perspective, where fascism originated, and how it linked to male sexuality. How does his description of the values of the Freikorps fit with the values and actions of the characters in *Starship Troopers*?

● *Hollow Man*

Verhoeven's most recent film disappointed many who were expecting a large-scale satire like *Starship Troopers*; although certainly not his best, it does actually prove fascinating when examined in the context of male desires and voyeurism. Caine is an arrogant scientist working on a drug that will produce invisibility; when he manages to make a gorilla disappear, he decides to test the drug on himself without telling his military superiors. Unfortunately, the drug doesn't seem to wear off and traps Caine in his invisible state. While the rest of his team attempt to find something to reverse the procedure, Caine begins to gradually break down. Never the most moral of men, his invisible state wrests him free of his inhibitions. This culminates in the rape of a woman he had previously watched undressing from his window and in the attempts of the scientists to trap him in the underground lab to prevent him from committing more crimes.

More than *Basic Instinct*, *Hollow Man* is a film about looking and the power that can give us 'a game about the watcher and the watched, and being caught out watching' (Ndalianis). On numerous occasions before invisibility, the camera's view becomes Caine's: notably when he is watching his female neighbour unconsciously undressing by her window; when she realises, and snaps closed the blinds, Caine says 'Dammit' ('on behalf of all the men in the audience', writes I Q Hunter, 2003). Voyeuristic pleasure has been initiated, desire has been teased, but then denied.

Once invisible and on the loose from the lab, Caine returns to the woman's apartment. It is hard to tell whether we are in his point of view, as he is invisible, as even if he was standing in front of the camera we would see right through to what both Caine and the spectator were denied earlier. Being a voyeur is no longer enough for Caine – though we can't see him, he attacks the woman and actualises his desire by raping her. From this point, Caine becomes a B-movie monster, stalking and slaying the scientists, 'killed' off about five times by the 'final girl' – but the point has been made. Male fantasies have been appealed to, and fulfilled … but then taken too far, breaking taboos. With his physical body seemingly vanished, there are no constraints for Caine's 'basic instincts', no tie to humanity. He becomes an almost purified form of juvenile masculinity: incredibly territorial, responding to his own insecurity with violence, and using the miracle drug for puerile voyeurism (the first thing he does is tweak a female assistant's nipple as she sleeps). Even in this B-movie, Verhoeven both appeals directly to male desires, then confronts the male spectator with an exaggerated and unpalatable depiction of those desires.

Key points to discuss:

● Look at the 'Men Viewing Violence' findings to how male audiences responded to the ambiguous 'rape' scene in *Basic Instinct*. How do they react to the (strongly suggested) rape scene in *Hollow Man*? Can they still identify with Caine?

- Compare the way in which *Basic Instinct* and *Hollow Man* both support Mulvey's ideas about male spectatorship and subvert them. Are the women merely passive objects of the gaze? Are the male spectator's desires fulfilled? Or is the gaze acknowledged, and made problematic?
- Watch *Rear Window* or *Body Double*. How do these films examine voyeurism? Do they work the same way as *Hollow Man*, making us identify with the spectator before shocking us with what the spectatorship reveals?

Ideas for further study

Examine other directors who address masculine identity or men's issues in cinema. Some interesting case studies might be:

- Neil LaBute: *In the Company of Men* (USA, 1997) and *Your Friends and Neighbours* (USA, 1999) particularly – analysing misogyny and male insecurity.
- Clint Eastwood: from *Unforgiven* (USA, 1992) and *Play Misty for Me* (USA, 1971), in which he deconstructs the tough cowboy/cop roles that brought him fame, to *Mystic River* (USA, 2002) where he examines masculine drives and relationships on a broader scale.
- Takeshi Kitano: like a Japanese Clint Eastwood, examining the driving forces of honour, integrity and aggression in men.

Glossary

Actualisation
The process by which we make our identity 'exist' in the material world – either through action, words or accumulation of wealth. Maslow lists this as a 'higher need'.

Androgyny
Blurring the line between masculine and feminine physical appearance/style, usually so the androgyne can achieve the most aesthetically appealing of both genders' appearance/style.

Auteur
French term for 'author' – applied by the *Cahiers du Cinéma* film critics to film directors who tended to have a personal style or who explored a set of personal themes. The term implies that a film is the result of a single individual's vision, in the same way as a novel is an author's singular vision.

Camp
The ironic adoption of deliberately exaggerated traditionally masculine or feminine traits.

Consumerism
The belief that happiness and fulfilment are attained through material wealth and the purchase and consumption/possession of products.

Determinism
Sociological theory that says personalities and roles are culturally produced.

Emasculation
The process by which a man's basic masculinity is removed. This could be physical, psychological or social.

Eroticisation
The process by which an object with no intrinsic sexual value is sexualised.

Essentialism
The belief that there is a basic, core masculinity and femininity within all men and women – beneath the socially constructed (and, it is implied, artificial) there is a 'real man' and 'real woman'.

Fetishisation

Literally, to attribute human traits to an inanimate object. In psychoanalysis, it is used to denote the process by which a source of fear, shame or anxiety is transformed into a source of pleasure. Laura Mulvey uses this to explain how male audiences respond to strong, active women on screen in order to 'protect' their sexual egos.

Functionalism

Sociological theory that says roles develop to fulfil certain functions in society.

Fundamentalism

Rejection of a complex, heterogenous worldview and the adoption of simple, essentialist and often traditional views.

Hegemony

The domination of one state over another. This can be interpreted culturally in the dominance of one ideological view. Louis Althusser went further to say that a hegemony was when the dominant class is able to persuade subordinate social groups not just to accept dominant ideology but to actually believe the existing social structure is to their benefit.

Heteroglossia

Russian critic Mikhail Bakhtin's name for texts that could harbour multiple meanings and interpretations.

Heteronormativity

A phrase, coined by Michael Warner, used in Queer theory to denote the way in which heterosexuality permeates every area of cultural, social and political – not just romantic and sexual – life and claims it as 'normal'.

Identification

The process in which the spectator emotionally engages with a character.

Machismo

Latino model of masculinity emphasising brotherhood, loyalty, male pride and honour. When negative, these traits can become an exaggerated, boastful manliness, where the suspicion of femininity can border on the misogynistic.

Masculinism

Unofficial term for a 'men's movement' that seeks to empower men in a world where many of the traditional lead roles are under threat. This can take the form of deconstructing phallocentric roles (in the style of feminism) or be more active, for instance in advancing father's legal rights.

Metrosexual

A breed of urban professional male who takes pleasure in his own appearance, without feeling as if he is any less masculine. It also implies a comfort with gay culture, and a generally more emotional approach to situations.

Mytho-poetic model
Essentialist view of masculinity, that maintains men have lost touch with the core, pre-industrial relationships and rituals they need to be balanced individuals.

New lad
A far more successful response, by media industries, to the failure by real men and women to accept the 'new man'. The new lad was not so much a return to traditional male values, but to a deliberately less threatening, more adolescent set of values, targeted by magazines like *Loaded* and *Maxim*.

New man
Unfocused term for an advertising initiative in the late 1980s that attempted to posit a man who adopted traditional feminine traits or roles. A predecessor of the 'metrosexual'.

New Queer cinema
Loose term for a group of early 1990s' gay male filmmakers who rejected models of 'acceptable' homosexuality with politically incorrect plots, and avant-garde structure and style.

Objectification
The process by which a human subject is reduced to having the status of an object.

Oedipus complex
Psychological development process, championed by Freud, in which the son fears the father and desires the mother; maturation occurs when, like Oedipus from Greek myth, the son 'kills' the father and is free to sexually claim the mother (or someone like her).

Patriarchy
Literally, a family controlled by the father; first used by Kate Millett to describe a social power structure based around men.

Phallocentric
A society or culture which is based around traditional male desire, as expressed symbolically by the phallus.

Postmodernism
Set of non-unified beliefs and aesthetic styles developed in response to modernism. Modernism attempted to find purity in aesthetic forms – postmodernism rejected this aim, and sought to mix the widest range of styles possible.

Queer theory
A theoretical approach to homosexuality that marks the gay experience and culture as intrinsically and immanently different to heteronormativity.

Reconstructed (male)
A man who has 'deconstructed' his masculinity to recognise where destructive or negative impulses originate and then 'put himself together again' – perhaps continuing to inhabit the same role but with more self-awareness.

Rite of passage

Originally a formal social/cultural ritual in which a boy endures some kind of physical or mental endurance test in order to prove himself worthy of manhood, now used to explain a significant event or stage in a person's life.

Scopophilia

Pleasure gained by watching. Discussed explicitly by Laura Mulvey.

Voyeurism

Pleasure gained by watching people who are not aware they are being watched.

References and resources

Selected Filmography

All That Heaven Allows (Douglas Sirk, USA, 1955)
American Beauty (Sam Mendes, USA, 1999)
American Pie (Paul Weitz, USA, 1999)
Basic Instinct (Paul Verhoeven, USA, 1992)
Carandiru (Hector Babenco, Brazil/Argentina, 2003)
Charlie's Angels: Full Throttle (McG, USA, 2003)
City of God (Fernando Meirelles, Brazil/France/USA, 2002)
Eddie Izzard: Dressed to Kill (Lawrence Jordan, UK, 1999)
Far from Heaven (Todd Haynes, USA, 2002)
Fight Club (David Fincher, USA, 1999)
Full Monty, The (Peter Cattaneo, UK, 1997)
Goldfinger (Guy Hamilton, UK, 1964)
Hollow Man (Paul Verhoeven, USA, 2000)
Motorcycle Diaries, The (Walter Salles, USA/Germany/France/Peru/Mexico/
    Argentina, 2004)
Lara Croft: Tomb Raider (Simon West, UK/Germany/USA/Japan, 2001)
My Best Friend's Wedding (P J Hogan, USA, 1997)
My Own Private Idaho (Gus Van Sant, USA, 1991)
Poison (Todd Haynes, USA, 1991)
Return, The (Andrei Zvyagintsev, Russia, 2003)
RoboCop (Paul Verhoeven, USA, 1987)
Safe (Todd Haynes, USA, 1995)
Simple Men (Hal Hartley, USA, 1992)
Starship Troopers (Paul Verhoeven, USA, 1997)
Tarnation (Jonathan Caouette, USA, 2004)
Time Out (Laurent Contet, France, 2001)
Total Recall (Paul Verhoeven, USA, 1990)
Trust (Hal Hartley, USA, 1990)

Velvet Goldmine (Todd Haynes, UK/USA, 1998)
Virgin Suicides, The (Sofia Coppola, USA, 1999)
Y tu mamá también (Alfonso Cuarón, Mexico, 2001)

Bibliography

J Berger, 1972, *Ways of Seeing*, Penguin

S Bliss, 1987, 'Revisioning Masculinity', *In Context*, Spring

R Bly, 1992, *Iron John*, Vintage

A Bouwer, 1999, 'Parody in *Starship Troopers*' in *Deep South* vol 3, available at www.otago.ac.nz/DeepSouth/1198/POP.html

J Butler, 1990, *Gender Trouble*: *Feminism and the Subversion of Identity*, Routledge

J F Codell, 1989, 'RoboCop: Murphy's Law, RoboCop's body and capitalism's work', *Jump Cut*, 34, 12–19

R W Connell, 1995, *Masculinities*, University of California Press

B DiStefano, 1998, 'Interview with Director Todd Haynes', *OutSmart*, November

T Doogan, 2000, 'Todd Doogan Interviews David Fincher' *DigitalBits*, 5/11/00, at www.thedigitalbits.com/articles/fightclub/fincherinterview.html

R Doyle, 1976, *The Rape of the Male*, Poor Richard's Press

B Ehrenreich, 1983, *Women in the Global Factory*, Boston South End Press

B Ehrenreich, 1995, *The Snarling Citizens: Essays*, Farrar, Strauss and Giroux

S Faludi, 1993, *Backlash: the Undeclared War against Women*, Vintage

W Farrell, 1974, *The Liberated Man*, Bantam Books

A Fernbach, 2000, 'The Fetishization of Masculinity in Science Fiction: The Cyborg and the Console Cowboy', *Science Fiction Studies*, vol. 27, July

C Gardner, 2003, 'Todd Haynes, Filmmaker' *Hollywood Reporter*, April 23

D Gilmore, 1991, *Manhood in the Making: Cultural Concepts of Masculinity*, Yale University Press

F Glass, 1989, 'The "New Bad Future": *RoboCop* and the 1980s' Sci-fi Films', *Science as Culture* no.5, 7–49

F Glass, 1990, 'Totally Recalling Arnold: Sex and Violence in the New Bad Future', *Film Quarterly* vol. 44 no. 1, Fall.

J Gray, 2002, *Men Are from Mars, Women Are from Venus*, HarperCollins

R Haddard, 1979, *Manifesto for the Men's Liberation Movement*, Free Men Inc

J Hearn, 1987, *The Gender of Oppression: Men, Masculinity and the Critique of Marxism*, St Martin's Press

I Q Hunter, 2003, 'Even Baser Instincts: Notes on *Hollow Man*'", *Intensities: The Journal of Cult Media*, no. 3, Spring, available at www.cultmedia.com/issue3/CMRhunter.htm

S Keen, 1992, *Fire in the Belly*, Bantam

M Kibby, 1996, 'Cyborgasm: Machines and Male Hysteria in the Cinema of the Eighties', *Journal of Interdisciplinary Gender Studies* Vol. 1, No. 2, September, 139–146, available at http://www.newcastle.edu.au/journal/jigs/issues/jigs1-2.html

X Mendick, 2002, 'The (un) Hollow Man', Kamera.co.uk, available at www.kamera.co.uk/interviews/paul_verhoeven.html

K Millett, 1977, *Sexual Politics*, Virago

J C Mitchell, 1998, 'Flaming Creatures: An Interview with Todd Haynes', *Filmmaker*, Fall, available at www.filmmakermagazine.com/fall1998/flaming_creatures.php

R Moore, 1991, *King, Warrior, Magician, Lover*, Harper San Francisco

M Moses, 1999, 'Fighting Words: An Interview with *Fight Club* Director David Fincher', at http://drdrew.com/DrewLive/article.asp?id=198

L Mulvey, 1975, 'Visual Pleasure and Narrative Cinema', originally published in *Screen* vol.16 no.3, Autumn, available at www.jahsonic.com/VPNC.html

A Ndalianis, 2001, 'Paul Verhoeven and His Hollow Men', *Screening the Past* no.13, December

A Oakley, 1972, *Sex, Gender and Society*, Vintage Books

A Oakley, 1974, *Woman's Work*, Vintage Books

C Paglia, 1991, *Sexual Personae*, Vintage Books

A Paredes, 1993, *Folklore and Culture of the Texan–Mexican Border*, University of Austin Press

L P Pedersen, 2001, *Understanding Masculine Personality Types*, Publish.com

K Phipps, 1998, '*Velvet Goldmine*', Onion A V Club at http://theavclub.com/feature/index.php?issue=3414&f=1

RSCG Worldwide Marketing, 2003, 'Metrosexuals: The Future of Men?' at www.behindthechair.com/displayarticle.aspx?ID=615&ITID=9

S Rowbotham, 1977, *Hidden from History*, Pluto

V Russo, 1981, *The Celluloid Closet*, HarperCollins

J Rutherford, 1988, *Male Order: Unwrapping Masculinity*, Lawrence and Wishart

P Schlesinger, 1998, 'Men Viewing Violence', available at www.fms.stir.ac.uk/mvv/violence.html

V Seidler, 1997, *Man Enough: Embodying Masculinities*, Sage

M Simpson, 2004, 'Here Come the Mirror Men', *The Independent*, 15 November

G Smith, 1999, 'Inside Out: One-on-one with David Fincher', *Film Comment*, September/October

C Stephens, 1995, 'Gentlemen Prefer Haynes', *Film Comment* vol 31, July/August

K Theweleit, 1989, *Male Fantasies* Volume 2*: Psychoanalyzing the White Terror*, University of Minnesota Press

R van Sheers, 1996, *Paul Verhoeven*, Faber

J Weeks, 1991, *Against Nature: Essays on History, Sexuality, and Identity*, Rivers Oram

P Wolf-Light, 1994, 'The Shadow of Iron John', *Men & Families*, no.17, Autumn

J Wyatt, Justin, 1998, 'Cinematic/Sexual: An Interview with Todd Haynes', *Film Quarterly*, Autumn. Available at http://home.comcast.net/~rogerdeforest/haynes/haynints.html

G Yudice, 1995, 'What's a Straight White Man to Do?', in C M Weems (ed), *Constructing Masculinity*, Routledge

Further reading

R Adams, (ed), 2002, *The Masculinities Studies Reader*, Blackwell Press

R W Connell, 1997, *Gender and Power: Society, the Person and Sexual Politics*, Stanford University Press

R W Connell, 2001, *The Men and the Boys*, University of California Press

W W Dixon, 2003, *Straight: Constructions of Heterosexuality in the Cinema*, State University of New York Press

S Ducat, 2004, *Wimp Factor: Gender Gaps, Holy Wars and the Politics of Anxious Masculinity*, Beacon Press

J K Gardiner (ed), 2002, *Masculinity Studies and Feminist Theory: New Directions*, Columbia University Press

D Gauntlett, 2002, *Media, Gender and Identity: An Introduction*, Routledge

M C Gutmann, 1996, *The Meanings of Macho: Being a Man in Mexico City*, University of California Press

C Holmland, 2001, *Impossible Bodies: Femininity and Masculinity at the Movies*, Taylor and Francis

B Hooks, 2003, *We Real Cool: Black Men and Masculinity*, Taylor and Francis

P Jackson *et al.* (ed), 1991, *Making Sense of Men's Magazines*, Polity Press

S Jeffords, 1993, *Hard Bodies: Hollywood Masculinity in the Reagan Era*, Rutgers University Press

P Lehman, 2001, *Masculinities: Bodies, Movies, Culture*, Routledge

B Pease (ed), 2002, *A Man's World? Changing Men's Practices in a Globalised World*, Zed Books

A Spicer, 2004, *Typical Men: Representation of Masculinity in Popular British Cinema*, I B Tauris

Y Tasker, 1993, *Spectacular Bodies: Gender, Genre and Action Cinema*, Routledge

S Whitehead (ed), 2002, *The Masculinities Reader*, Polity Press

Useful websites

www.aber.ac.uk/media/ – very useful starting point for students

www.achillesheel.free.uk/ – website of the men's movement magazine with archive

www.channel4/film/ – good film site

www.ejumpcut.org/ – very good archives of reviews and criticism

www.filmunlimited.com – *The Guardian*'s film site and archive

www.foxmovies.com/fightclub/ – the official website for *Fight Club*

www.genderads.com – fantastic resource for representations/ideologies in advertising

www.imagesjournal.com/ – alternative film site

www.imdb.com – invaluable for facts and user opinions

www.kamera.co.uk – a good alternative, academic yet accessible film site

www.mensactivism.org/ – background to men's movement plus up-to-date news

www.menstuff.org/ – well-organised site for men's issues

www.menweb.org/ – comprehensive site exploring male issues

www.outrate.net – general gay site, but with good introduction to New Queer cinema

www.paulverhoeven.net – official site for Paul Verhoeven

www.qcinema.com/ – another good introduction to gay cinema

www.queertheory.com/ – good for defining what this branch of theory is

www.rottentomatoes.com – good alternative film site

www.screenonline.org.uk

www.senseofcinema.com – very good academic film site

www.theory.org.uk – rigorous yet accessible site to introduce students to theory

www.un-real.co.uk – Unorthodox Reel's alternative film site

www.worldfilm.about.com

Acknowledgements

There are many people who assisted directly in the writing of this guide, and many whose comments and ideas helped develop my own over the years.

Firstly, I'd like to thank Vivienne Clark, my editor, for her advice and guidance; for rewording my somewhat 'elliptical' phrasing; and for liquid inspiration on the South Bank. I also owe many thanks for the staff and students of Seven Kings High School, especially Jo Amphlett for her endless support, and my Year 13 students for their youthful perspective on gender.

Thanks to my family, especially Mum and Dad, for raising me in an environment where 'being a man' was always a topic for discussion rather than a simple expectation.

And extra special thanks to my lovely Emma, for her support, her endless enthusiasm, understanding and intelligence, and for loving 'disturbing' films as much as I do.